THE LAST STUPID CHURCH BOOK YOU'LL EVER READ

TWO CHRISTIANS TAKE A LOOK AT THE LUCRATIVE MEDIUM OF ORGANIZED RELIGIOSITY

THE LAST STUPID CHURCH BOOK YOU'LL EVER READ

TWO CHRISTIANS TAKE A LOOK AT THE LUCRATIVE MEDIUM OF ORGANIZED RELIGIOSITY

BY
BENJAMIN SAMPLES
JAMES TOWNSEND

SCB

STUPID CHURCH BOOK PRESS
CHARLESTON

www.stupidchurchbook.com

NOTE: If you purchased this book without a cover, you should be aware that this book has no cover. It was reported as having "no cover" to the publisher, and neither the authors nor the publisher have received any cover for this "cover-less" book.

This is not a work of fiction. Except for the fake parts. Which aren't works of non-fiction.

THE LAST STUPID CHURCH BOOK YOU'LL EVER READ

A Stupid Church Book Press...Book
Charleston, West Virginia

www.stupidchurchbook.com

Jacket and illustrations designed by Austin Boyd.

ISBN-13: 978-0-9817600-0-1
ISBN-10: 0-9817600-0-7

LCCN: 2008904098

First edition: June 2008

Printed in the United States of America.

9 8 7 6 5 4 3 2 1 0

Cover

Story

Title

STUPID CHURCH BOOK HYPE

Follow up

Marketing

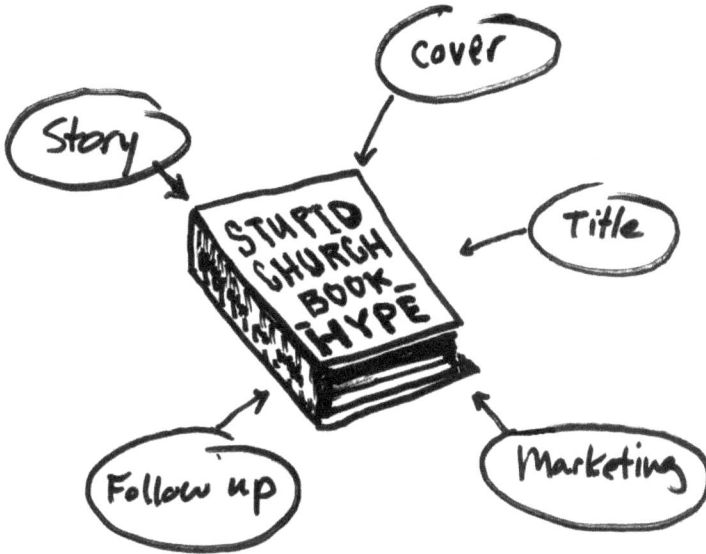

AND FIRST, A WORD FOR OUR SPONSORS

We don't have a problem with *all* church books.

Just the **stupid** ones.

The authors who write these books tell you that your life will be complete once you read these books of theirs. If it isn't, just buy their workbook or journal or discovery CD, and that should take you through the process pretty well.

But the truth is, your life probably won't improve that much from reading any of these books.

And we can't guarantee you a very significant life-change from reading ours either. In fact, we don't even think *that* should be the goal of a good book.

We can't make you a better person. We can't make you richer. We can't give you purpose.

So we're not promising that.

We're just promising to be completely honest with what we've found in the culture of Christianity today.

And what we've found is a marketing-scheme that could make the secular commercial industry blush with envy. As Christians, we come from a pretty sturdy tradition of folks having problems with marketplaces being set up in the church. In fact, this protest against marketing salvation goes all the way back to Jesus.

We just wanted to talk a little in this book about our journeys through all the realms of Christian marketing: the books, the music, the church services themselves. It's all a result of our personal experiences and observations.

We've read the stupid church books. We've heard the stupid songs and sermons. . .

And we still think the Bible has so much more to offer.

~James

ACKNOWLEDGEMENTS

for those exploited with false words
from the greedy

for those whose ears are itching

YOUR PURCHASES

TRANSACTION CONTINUES→

NO RETURNS W.O. RECEIPT

stu·pid / styu-/ *adjective,* **-er, -est,** *noun*

— *adjective*

1. lacking ordinary quickness and keenness of mind; dull.
2. characterized by or proceeding from mental dullness; foolish; senseless.
3. tediously dull, esp. due to lack of meaning or sense; inane; pointless.
4. annoying or irritating; troublesome.
5. in a state of stupor; stupefied.
6. *Slang.* excellent; terrific.

— *noun*

7. *Informal.* a stupid person.

How It
. . .Almost Was

Hi, my name is Clancy Wiggum.

Several times a week, I spend the day in a world that many others will never experience:

Jail.

Those who have been subjected to it surely wish they never had; those who currently reside there most definitely wish they were somewhere else. For many, it was easy to gain admittance — dealing to an undercover officer, refusing to run during a heist gone bad, slicing about in a drunken rage, or pinning down an innocent child; however, for the few who will gain it, the right of exit is a long fought struggle, earned through a painful combination of emotional solitude, physical clashes, unadulterated fear, and a lot of luck.

Incidentally, the majority will never leave these

dark, musty halls.

Ironically located deep within the mountains of a town called "Liberty," the C.M. Burns State Penitentiary is a maximum-security prison housing the most ruthless criminals in the state. Escape is virtually impossible. Reinforced concrete walls surround the entire complex while multiple rungs of razor wire are weaved into the 20-foot-tall fences that outline individual compounds. Guard towers stand at small intervals around the perimeter, discouraging any thought of a breakout. Passage through the earth under the walls would also prove hopeless as the prison grounds rest firmly on a foundation of solid rock, the remnant of an abandoned slate mine.

The closest town, Springfield, is home to the Springfield College of Christian Studies. I taught there after I finished a stint with the Army Rangers. Recently, the penitentiary and the school have assembled an on-site educational program for inmates to pursue a bachelor's degree. After hearing about the opportunity to serve on the grounds, though apprehensive, I was anxious to assist. I met the prisoners for the first time when I proctored an entrance test for the courses. Now, I teach in the prison as an adjunct professor of mathematics and Biblical weights and measures.

Journey with me to the educational facilities, located in the middle of the yard, far inside the prison's walls, and amongst the inmates. As you wait in the front lobby, the tales of inmate riots disperse an enduring chill through the small of your back that remains with you long after you leave this surreal environment.

the tales of inmate riots disperse an enduring chill through the small of your back

Through small, cloudy windows, I can vaguely make out a few figures, inhabitants of this foreign society.

The names of the "pods," the prisoner housing sections, are named after past officers and wardens that have been injured or killed during inmate uprisings. After a prison in the northern part of the state shut down, transfers left Burn's Pen extremely over-crowded and under-staffed. Still, the area is carefully arranged so that the prisoners can see neither beyond the walls nor into adjacent buildings. A labyrinth of halls and walkways lead to my classroom; it is blocked intermittently by heavy steel doors and guarded checkpoints. In total, nine doors stand between my destination and me, between the fresh air of freedom and the stale stench of captivity.

Though I am accompanied by two guards, they are armed only with nightsticks.

They warned me, "Don't let your guard down.

You must maintain physical and emotional dominance at all times."

The traverse across the open yard inevitably triggers a degree of uneasiness. The stare you receive from inmates instantly marks you as an outsider. The facilities run rampant with disease and violence. By the end of the first month I found myself in the ER with a staph infection.

Walking down the last set of stairs, you see the students lined up, eagerly awaiting the day's activities. For them, part of the lure of taking a course is the prospect of sitting in a class uncuffed and un-chained.

I found out later that over half of my students are lifers, mostly for single or multiple homicides or gang murders.

Lately, I have noticed the same gentleman always standing at the front of the line. I would like to introduce you to Louis Leggs, a sturdy, mustachioed individual of Italian descent, serving time for a double-murder during an exchange of illegal narcotics. As he entered class the first day, he eyed me down and approached me.

Several others quickly gathered within earshot.

The guards were busy contending with some other inmates who were causing a distraction a few meters away.

I was surrounded.

And I was alone.

"Dey told us you was one a dose churchy folks. But you got fightin' hands Mr. Wiggum. I'll bet you a fighter."

Fight or flight.

My first instinct — *Quick, where are the exits? None. . .*

My heart begins to race.

I looked down at my hands, palms up — the same way I do sometimes during worship. I lean in and reveal with a now instinctive austerity:

"Sir, I was trained as a killer. But now these hands work for Christ."

Mr. Leggs paused, glanced over to his peers then back at me. He nodded, apparently in acceptance of what I said, and continued into class; the others followed suit. The confrontation was over.

Exhale... Ahhhh. . .Relief.

I later related my service in the Army and how I had come to know the Lord while I was a P.O.W. in Iraq, all of which appeared quite interesting to the students. Sometimes I use military or Christian examples in solving problems. During one such instance, we were using algebra to simultaneously determine the amounts of swords, spears, and bows that a Roman military commander received from a weapons smith during the fall of Jerusalem.

Mr. Leggs interrupted, "Mr. Wiggum, won't da warden let you bring in any visual aides?"

"I tried, but they made me check them at the door."

The group chuckled.

Louis replied, "Dey made me check **everything** at da door!"

The others agreed in laughter. "Yeah, me too!" "And me!"

"Okay okay, let's get back to our task at hand."

Other times I will use business examples; unquestionably though, I always use real-world examples and I always make them a challenge.

The thing that must be understood about this society is that no one in here believes they will stay here for life. Recently, Mr. Leggs and I have had the opportunity to talk one on one. *Mono a mono* he would tell you.

His thick accent exposes him immediately:

"Man, ya know when dey brought me down to Liberty from Shelbyville, I thought dis could come er go, but when dey took me out to Burn's Pen, it really kicked in. I knew I was here for the long haul. But hey, der's still a chance, right?"

They hope.

It is all they have.

It is all any of us have.

I think of Paul and all the time he spent behind walls in conditions probably worse than these. It's the little things like experiencing a small dose of reality or overcoming tough problems that fuel hope. From time to time I am able to give them small glimpses of hope.

And I am able to share the hope I have because of He who works within me.

During the early stages of his stay here at Burn's Pen, Louis spent over 29 months in lock-up for various infractions. That equates to over 850 days in guarded, 24-hour solitary confinement. It must feel great to converse.

"So, Mr. Wiggum, what's your plans? You ain't always gonna teach us felons are ya?"

I relayed to Louis my plan of starting a post-modern, missional, emergent, Christ-following church with the hope of ministering in prisons all over the country; I could tell his interests were piqued.

A few weeks passed.

One day after class, Louis asked me to sit down with him.

Strewn across the table, he displayed his plan: a seminary-type of degree through distance learning, a line of appeals that may lead to his release, and a loophole; apparently, in Shelbyville, one felony can be forgiven allowing an individual to serve the remainder of his sentence in a religious organization under electronic monitoring.

He is intent on pursuing the degree and hopefully returning one day to his home in Shelbyville to begin a similar type of endeavor.

Our time with swords and algebra started out as an edgy exchange of guarded bravado. Today, though both sides remain civil, I suppose the air still has an amount of sion in it. Realistically, it is not likely that Mr. Leggs will ever leave Burn's Pen. Louis and the two million others serving time in prisons across the country exist in a civilization far separated from where we live today.

it's not likely that Mr. Leggs will ever leave Burn's Pen

The distance between the yard and the parking lot is so much wider than the walls that separate them.

This order, surely the opposite of society, is a world often cast aside — one that free citizens

8

may speak of, but truly know very little about.

From behind his thick glasses, Mr. Leggs' eyes reveal a renewed strength. I remember the first time I saw him, angry and aggressive. He would often sit in the back corner of the classroom. With the challenges of my course laid before him, he has become a new man. Louis looks forward to class as a time *Louis looks forward to class as a time of civility and respect* of civility and respect in an otherwise embarrassing, dangerous, and worrisome existence.

Since classes have begun, he has not spent a single day in lock-up.

During one of my monthly reviews with the prison administration, word came from the chaplain that one evening after our course, Louis had accepted the Lord.

Now, he even tutors and assists some of his fellow inmates and leads a worship service inside the prison.

Last Thursday, I asked him to the board, handed him the dry erase marker, and though the guards weren't even in the room, I took his seat among the others while he finished explaining to the class one of the particularly tough questions we were working on.

As we have worked together within these confines, as we have struggled through tests and quizzes, and as we have talked about life, we have learned to appreciate and admire each other as fellow men.

Louis is undergoing a spiritual metamorphosis.

I cannot honestly say that I initiated it. Perhaps it would have occurred and continued whether or not I was present. What I am sure about is that it would not have happened if no one were there. I take solace in the fact that I was at least able to experience it and only hope I had some hand in it.

Several weeks ago, Louis and I talked about class and how the students were receiving me as an instructor.

He encouraged me with the following explanation:

"Mr. Wiggum, dese guys won't let ya know if you were helping them. In dese walls, dey can't. You gotta *think* dat what you do helps just in case it really does; you'd hate to have known you *coulda* helped someone earlier but dat now der's no time. Dat's why ya do what you do."

I asked, "Louis, what else can I do?"

His final statement sticks:

"Clancy, JUST DO YOU."

A Consumer Report:
Behind Closed Doors

Isn't that a nice story?

"JUST DO YOU."

Lots of struggle, redemption, people turning their lives around.

We love stuff like that.

But, sad to say, the story you just read about old Clancy Wiggum just isn't true.

Just a bunch of fluff.

Like most of the other religious books we tend to go after.

There are so many books today that contain the kind of heart-lifting, inspiring junk you just enjoyed reading in the first chapter of this Stupid Church Book.

Do you ever just walk the Christian section of your bookstore and find yourself a little overwhelmed by the innumerable titles that fill each shelf to the point of structural compromise? Or better yet, for a more condensed example, go to an exclusively Christian bookstore and find yourself in the same situation?

What's more, these books will all have something different to tell you. If one says the key to success is positive thinking, another one right beside it will tell you that you need to face facts and stop thinking beyond your limits.

And worse still, you can't just stop with the book.

You then have to buy the study guide, the journal, the calendar, the church group resource, the Scripture guide, the video, the ministry toolbox, the seminars, the health guide, the coffee mug, the coaster, the cheap bracelet, the bumper sticker, the place mat, the key chain, the toilet paper. . .

Have you noticed a trend?

It's hard to get past the feeling, which feels like oil slicked over life-giving water, that we're all being had. Pastors and teachers write a book that, by and large, says nothing in particular, and then franchise that book into countless other avenues, making money off of every one. This money goes into sponsoring even more themed events like seminars, conferences, videos and church resources. The money from those events, and all subsequent profits, then go into the appropriate pockets. It has become a perpetual act of self-preservation.

How did our faith, and our churches, become so consumer-based?

How is it that financial schemes and business ethics are now perfectly applicable to our lives as Christians?

How is it that we have allowed our pastors and shepherds to see their flocks as, first and foremost, consumers?

What we are encountering today is the "consumerizing" of Christianity.

Churches are taking anything that makes a buck in the secular arena, then proscribing the word "Christian" to it, and marketing it to the sacred masses. Biblical truths are too often weighed against the opinions of "the consumer."

"Should our teachers teach this?"

"Should our pastors say this?"

The answers to these, and other "should" questions hang on one central question:

Will what we have to say please the consumer?

Or, in other words, if we say or do something this Sunday, will the consumer be back next Sunday?

Even the motives are corrupt. Salvation takes a backseat to the dollar. Church leaders do not always want the consumer back for purposes of salvation or edification. Instead, these leaders know that if something is said this week which doesn't tickle the ears of a customer in a positive fashion, then the church will lose out on that customer's money.

But this is not an abstract conclusion. I have encountered this time after time. I have discussed theology and doctrine with pastors, only to have the pastor say, when the conversation is done, "Well that may be all well and good, but we can't say that in church. People will leave!"

That Doggy in the Window

I grew up in a Nazarene church. Being a guitar player, when the church decided to try and move into the more contemporary sphere of worship — when we were simply "contempi-curious" — I naturally volunteered my services.

This was an extremely hard transition for the congregation. There was a healthy mix of people who welcomed the modern change, and there were those who wanted to stay with the piano and just sing traditional hymns.

One couple in the congregatoin remarked how he could do without the "bar music" in church.

Now I'm not a very fancy person. I don't play dress up very often, and have lived my life thus far quite content with the corduroy pants and black button-up shirt routine. So when I started playing with this church in my normal attire, I quickly found myself, along with the praise team, in a pastor's conference one Sunday night after service.

The pastor wanted to share a "progress report" on how he thought the contemporary transition was coming along.

The first subject he brought up was attire.

"Sunday morning," he said, "is our *sales window*. When someone walks in who has never been to our church before, what they see, on stage and in the congregation, is basically what we're offering."

The praise team nodded in agreement.

"So," he continued, "when we get up there with ratty clothes, not looking our best, what kind of message do you think that sends? People wearing suits attract people wearing suits, and people wearing ratty clothes, well. . ."

The worship team finished for him, ". . .attract people wearing ratty clothes."

If I were a more aggressive person, perhaps I would have thrown my coffee in his face and stormed out.

If I had it to do over again, I probably would.

But back then, I just nodded my head and listened, and the nastiness of that philosophy didn't occur to me until much later. Maybe God didn't allow me to see the nastiness at the time because He doesn't like me throwing coffee in people's faces.

15

But it is within these discussions, within these "Pastors' Parables," so to speak, that we find the heart of modern churches.

It's all about the sales window.

It's about attracting the right kind of person. And God is no longer the judge of who those "right people" are. Their financial status and the quality of their dress determine their status in the church and in Christian life.

Jesus told parables about God accepting people from all walks of life. Today, pastors tell parables about rejecting certain people for statistical reasons.

These discussions, these business meetings, happen all the time behind closed church doors. And they will keep happening. And these pastors will keep getting what they have wanted all along: fat wallets and plastic smiles.

+ + +

Hopefully you are beginning to get a glimpse of what I mean by the "consumerizing" of Christianity.

At its most ugly point, it is seeing the Church that God founded in Jesus as nothing more than a business-oriented "product-provider." It is seeing the souls that He came to reconcile to God as "consumers." And it is seeing God not as a Person, but as a "function," which must be changed or manipulated as the demands of consumers change and grow. And there are many different levels, or degrees, of the consumerization of Christianity.

The form that we are seeing today validates the words of the apostle Paul, written about two thousand years ago.

16

In his first letter to Timothy, Paul instructs the young Christian leader to preach the Word. He also tells him to correct, rebuke, and encourage. "For," he says, "the time will come when they will not endure sound doctrine." Instead, to satisfy their own wants and desires, they will bring around them a great number of teachers to say what their "itching ears" want to hear. (I Timothy 4:3)

Paul said it first.

Then Peter said something like it. Check out 2 Peter, chapter 2.

There has never been a moment in history before now where there have been more people like this. They want to hear only those things which please, justify, and fulfill their selfish motives. If anything can be said about churches today, it is that many of our preachers and leaders are very skilled in the art of saying what peoples' itching ears want to hear.

And I have had enough.

I've had enough of subjugating the gospel to political correctness, of a capitalistic Christianity more concerned with running a business and attaining personal prosperity over anything else. I've had enough of Christian leaders marketing empty words and digging empty wells, then selling these fables to the needy masses at record-breaking volume.

I've also had enough of hip "emerging" leaders putting on different outfits and doing the same thing, but calling it a "conversation."

And I hope that you've had enough as well.

I also want to point beyond this commerciality to a more authentic relationship with Jesus. Too many times, it seems that what we call "church" today actually *hinders* our relationship with God, instead of

17

helping it. Therefore it is my prayer to relentlessly pursue the truth as it is found in Jesus, to examine and confront whatever trials may fall upon the Church to which we all belong, and to encourage where God has shown me to encourage. It is also my prayer that you will extend to me the same courtesy.

And may we all do our best not to scratch itching ears.

Now, then:

Let's make some noise.

The *Nesses* and the *Hows* of it All

There are, perhaps among others, three notions that drive most of us to religious musings. In other cases, these same notions may hinder us from such.

These are the notions of *smallness*, *usefulness*, and *uniqueness*. It's interesting how the same reality, when perceived by diverse groups of people, can be seen in very different ways.

The seeming smallness of our existence in this universe, for instance, may lead one person to speculate about whether this does, in fact, conceal a much deeper *bigness*. Thus this person finds himself or herself being drawn into one religious tradition or another.

Or perhaps the same notion drives another to purchase a large amount of crystals to wear around one's neck, for energy alignment reasons which are, let's face it, sometimes only obvious to the person wearing them. They will spend the rest of their life bouncing from one metaphysical New-Age philosophy to another, wondering why the reiki is not very effective on their bum knee, and how come, with all their meditation classes, they still end up flipping off the bad driver in front of them.

And yet another person may be driven by the same notion into a complete naturalistic atheism, which leaves them only to become, quite literally, material boys and girls living in a material world. They usually go on to become quite "educated" in matters of religion, which really only means they accumulate a number of learned responses, which are witty enough in their own right, with which they may disarm the religious notions of the rest of humanity.

But any way you cut it, we find ourselves here, seemingly small creatures living on a seemingly insignificant planet in the middle of a very big universe.

We look up at the stars or out over vast landscapes and harbor certain thoughts concerning our smallness with respect to the universe and all its parts.

We've all felt it.

Driving from one big city to another, you're confronted with spans of quiet earth, whose geography and lifeline is shadowed under a midnight sky whose stars are still walled out by the peripheral light of nearby towns. The darkness of an interstate at night, in the middle of a lonely stretch of country road or grassland, can be quite unsettling. The same goes for the canyons, mountains, oceans and forests which we all, as humans, love to frequent.

Perhaps we love to see bigness because of our inner struggles with smallness. We love going to the Grand Canyon, Niagara Falls, or seeing the Seqoiuas, because it implies a certain bigness out there. Some being incomprehensibly bigger than ourselves appears to have orchestrated all of this.

20

And somehow this comforts us.

It must comfort us. Or else these places of vastness wouldn't be tourist attractions. They would be places to avoid at all costs.

This incredible vastness of the universe, by default, leads our conceptually driven minds straight to God. That's what Paul means, in Romans, when he says that no one is really blind to God's existence. The entire universe is struck through with a signature of His glory.

And this notion of smallness takes us right into the question of our *usefulness*. Because whether you're driving along these lonesome country roads I've mentioned, interrupted by the occasional trailer or farmhouse, or finding yourself packed like sweaty sardines in traffic jams between towering skyscrapers, it's easy to question our usefulness in creation. We begin to wonder about whether our lives here have any meaning, or if we're just specks of dust on the cosmic curtain.

Society, and our modern way of life, does nothing to help matters.

We've fashioned for ourselves, with an almost diabolical motivation, the most dehumanizing jobs that we can think of. There may be nothing more disconcerting than sitting in your cubicle day after day, tapping out months or years of your life to the rhythm of clacking keys, and still trying to feel unique and empowered. Because really, in a cubicle, it's often easier to feel just the opposite: run-of-the-mill and completely powerless. We were never meant to waste our lives staring at computer screens fifty floors up. No matter how many audio books you may be able to fit on an mp3 player, it won't do much to hide the fact that a fallen humanity can come up with pretty crappy ways of doing things.

Moreover, all of this leads to a very accurate observation:

We don't run the show.

The question which follows, however, is, does anyone?

Again, the bombardment of these *nesses* may lead us all into very different territories. But one thing is for sure: lots of things have gone terribly wrong, and none of us are in much of a position to change things, beyond recycling, carpooling, and eating plenty of soluble fiber.

There are thousands upon thousands of philosophical systems and situations that explore our understanding of eternal existence and where we fit in with it all as Christians. For each of these there are at least as many books that illustrate how to find yourself there, the *hows*.

Here are some I like:

how to live	*with purpose*
how to face death	*with dignity*
how to handle the loss of your loved ones	*with hope*
how to handle the birth of your child	*with an epidural*
how to raise your kids	*haphazardly*
how to save your marriage or save your money	*can't have both*
how to handle your divorce	*with oven mits*
how to date	*zealously*
how to not date	*kiss it goodbye*
how to break up or how to love	*but not be in love*
how to witness	*cheesily*
how to read the Bible	*or the next best paraphrase*
how to worship	*hands up, palms outward please*
how to pray	*heads bowed, eyes closed*
how to study	*or pretend to*
how to get closer to God	*or act like it*
how to get your family closer to God	*or pretend they are*

how to be successful	*or go broke*
how to handle your boss	*with a baseball bat*
how to handle your workers	*with bullwhips*

And if there isn't a book that covers each of these life events, there is surely a small group session at church that performs a similar function.

Most of the time there are both.

Those of you who are less fortunate will have to make due with hearing it from the pastor. It might be possible to read every one of the books, or at least sit in with all the small groups. In the "emerging church," the groups are normally named something more catchy like "core teams," "discovery groups," "cells," etc. Or possibly, over time, one could catch all the topics during sermons.

With all these different avenues though, folks should certainly be able to find the cure for what ails them. You are told the answers to all your questions are there if you look for them (and seek them!).

The quotes begin to flow:

"I can do all things through Christ who strengthens me,"

"Ask and it will be given,"

etc., etc., ad hominem, no end 'em.

I'm no longer satisfied with a particular book's message just because it has *apparent* Scriptural support for every point made. Every message out there, although contradicting one another, is supposedly backed up by countless half-referenced, contextually-impaired Scripture quotes.

I think it's time we asked ourselves, has "commentary" on Scripture overrun Scripture itself?

And in case you should ever feel helpless during the special times in your life, there is always the little devotional book for any of a million subjects: success or happiness, failure or sadness, reread them, shelve 'em.

They are perfect for gifts, right?

You are told of the Biblical principles and strategies that will free you: financial freedom, debt success, purpose-driven driving, purpose-driven tithing.

After all, God can do more with your 10% than you can with 100%, right?

And for all of you reverse-tithers out there, those who give 90% and only keep 10%, just imagine what He can do with your 90%! If everyone reverse-tithed, we'd have more mega-churches than Wal-Marts!

Scary, huh?

Stop Reading the Comics and Laugh at the News

The sweet aroma of sizzling bacon and sausage reaches my nose before her voice reaches my ears:

"Rise and shine! Time to give God the glory!"

Not unlike any other Sunday, I rolled over, still in my PJs, and headed downstairs where a breakfast fit for a king awaited me. Dad sat at the table, folding up the Sunday paper and setting it to the side. Mom joined us with several last minute preparations — salt, pepper, some butter, and hopefully some chocolate milk.

As we ate, Dad would share some story he had just read about in the *Today* section of the paper.

One story that stands out is that of the capture of rogue graffiti artist, Stewart Quagmire, whose "art" had shown itself all over town. You could find his work on bridge supports, retaining walls, buildings, sidewalks, fences, dumpsters — anything you could spread paint on. He later admitted to police that his misleading signature, "Stewie Q.," was intended to throw off investigators. It may have worked had he not committed one fatal flaw. The single subject of his graffiti was very well represented.

So well represented that it was used to capture the criminal responsible: Stewie had been painting self-portraits all over town!

After finishing breakfast, I normally had a little extra time before I had to get ready for church. I always went hunting through the thick Sunday paper trying to find the comics — which were normally holed-up amongst the grocery store advertisements and coupons.

First, *Garfield*.

Then *Family Circus*, followed by either *Peanuts* or *Hi and Lois*.

I always saved *The Far Side* for last.

My plan was really pretty simple:

1. Hope for a good start.
2. Add some decent filler.
3. Crescendo with the grand finale.

Isn't that how we approach church these days?

With the comics, more often than not, though, I was let down. Maybe a smirk, or at most, an audible *hmph!*, but never anything life changing.

A Tour through the Double Doors

Let's take a look at the "Christianity" many people encounter. This probably won't prove such an uncommon scenario:

It's Sunday morning, around 9:30 or so. The pews are intricately shaped oak, topped by a comfortable red cushion of sorts.

Or orange.

It's up to you, really.

The windows have that tint that, in case you were wondering, really lets you know you're in church. The carpet is new, very clean.

You can smell it.

It's delicious, if you are into that new-carpet smell.

From the ceilings hang globe lights, and a couple of fans are spinning in case the preacher or semi-contemporary priest gets rolling. Double doors lead into the sanctuary where, if you were to walk down the aisle formed by the pews you would find yourself standing in front of an altar and the pulpit.

Here there be flowers.

Some more culturally-savvy churches may have done away with the altar or the pulpit.

Then, as you slowly raise your head, you see the chairs that are for the choir.

Perhaps a chancel.

And behind them, perhaps a baptistery. The cool churches normally have the "band" area off to the left or right. If it is a long-established church, there will have, in the history of said church, been an intense civil war over the question of transitioning into a "contemporary" style of worship, with the "old folks" siding with the "old hymns" played solely on the "old piano," and the younger crowd quite ready for at least an acoustic guitar or two. So don't take this band area lightly. Lots of sweat and tears, and maybe even blood, went into getting that drum set there.

Finally, as you look to the ceiling, you see a large, probably life-sized, wooden cross hanging from a white wall. Sometimes the cross is found subdued in an abstract piece of art. A lone keyboard, piano, or maybe even an organ rings throughout the congregation as the men sing their part of the hymn and the women lightly harmonize the chorus as each verse ends.

Often, the hymns of old have been replaced by the hymns of those new harbingers of heavenly music such as Matt Redman, deleriou5?, or others.

During worship, a hand is lifted as a tear rolls down the song leader's cheek. The music rises and falls. More experienced worship leaders may attempt the "spirit-spin," waving his or her arms around as they do circles on the stage that would make the best of ballet dancers sigh with envy.

It is soon time for prayer and fellowship around the altar. A lady in the back stands and asks the believers to pray for her husband, that he may be saved. Together, the congregation kneels and prays for the requests. Everyone then raises and returns to their seats. After the next hymn, an older fellow stands up and tells the congregation how the Lord has been so good to him this week. Shortly after, a soft instrumental is played while ushers prepare and pray for the offering ceremony. At times, a guest singer or music group comes and presents several selections for the congregation.

It's possible you grew up with the people around you.

They are the kids you have attended school with, their parents, or your own grandparents, siblings, or children. You've went places with them and had dinner with them. They still sit in the same places. Some are older members, some have left and returned, some are new faces who just moved from another state. Maybe you have just moved there. A young couple brings their child and he whimpers from time to time throughout the service.

As the preacher comes, dressed either in a suit and tie or casual slacks and slick sweater (mostly pastels), he announces the Scripture so that all can be looking through their Bibles to find the verses.

Again, the hip churches have capitalized on technology and project the words on some scenic vista on one of the projector screens in the front. These are also the churches that are able to produce those "passion plays" during Easter that feature an actual long-haired-Crest-using-resurrection-flying-transfiguring-in-all-His-glory-Jesus, who looks more like he belongs to U2 than first century Israel.

When the pastor (lead teacher, in said hip churches) reaches the pulpit, there is some cliché comic relief about the weather or the countenance of the crowd, or perhaps a top-ten list relating God to golfing, and then he asks that all bow their heads for a word of prayer. After the "amen," the verses are read as the preacher removes his suit jacket and loosens his collar.

It's go-time.

For the sermon, there are at least two options: the "old" way, and the "modern" way.

The Old Way

If the church is a proponent of option one, the "old way," the preacher may begin with a short testimonial. For these conventional services it may proceed as follows:

He reminds, with tears in his eyes, "I've been saved for twenty-three years and it just keeps getting better and better!"

Or, conversely, he warns, "I've been saved for twenty-three years and it just keeps getting harder and harder!"

Or some preachers stick with old faithful, "You wanna know my only regret? Why did I wait till I was forty-five years old to get saved?"

This is normally followed by a fundamental assortment of steps.

Primarily, there is some background on the "character" contained in the Scripture. The next step deals with relating the situation to an age of computers and evil. There is customarily a statement or two about the devil devouring our youth or about money, *the* root of all evil. The closing illustrations deal with how we need to get back to the way it used to be. And finally, around 11:45, there is the infamous altar call where you, too, can be saved.

> *with every head bowed, every eye closed,*
> (in case something magical happens)
> *no one is going to call you out or anything,*
> *if you feel that you want to be saved,*
> *could you just raise your hand?*
> *it's that easy*
> (pause)
> *okay, there's one, bless you,*
> *do we have another?*
> (pause)
> *won't you come?*
> (pause)
> *well, if the song leader and pianist will come,*
> *we'll have a song in closing. . .*

For a couple reasons, there is usually one more song. This is because the person has not yet come to the altar and they need another chance before, as the pastor suggests, they go out that very night and get hit by a train, or because someone has come, been prayed with, and now we can all rejoice with our new brother or sister.

Hopefully the one who raised his hand during the "altar call" was sincere and will live out the calling for fellowship that Jesus initiated. Provided, that is, that anyone raised their hand at all. Often times these emotionally charged instances are at least directed, if not totally manipulated, by the church leaders.

A Side Story

For years I played guitar in a ministry group which toured various churches. We did revivals, youth retreats, and other musically hip events.

At the time, the group consisted of about eleven people. We were headed up by a "manager," who booked our gigs, and basically did the "preaching" while we played the music. We would play the songs, and he would run around the sanctuary or venue screaming and urging the audience to stand up, clap their hands, hug each other, or some other typical musical/church interaction.

I remember one time, when we were playing a church in Missouri, we were doing the song "Love Can Build A Bridge." By this time I had been in the group long enough to know what was going on regarding audience manipulation.

Going in with sincerity, I now saw that what many people called a "move of the Spirit" was in truth only emotional responses to cliché musical phrasings and chord progressions.

Our leader would pump up the congregation all the time.

During this one performance in Missouri, as we were playing the love-bridge-building song, we reached a high point in the performance. People were crying, holding hands and swaying. At this point, our leader turned around to face us in the middle of one of his emotional speeches, gave us a thumbs-up, and winked at us.

I was blown away!

It was as if he was saying, "We got 'em, guys!"

I quit the group when we got back from Missouri.

The Modern Way

The sermon option concerning the "modern" congregations, if not completely replaced by house groups or the like, has more of a coffee shop feel and focuses more on relating with people in school or the workplace, and aligning your finances with Christian goals. Last week I attended a church that actually had a coffee shop adjoined to the foyer (you couldn't take your beverage into the "holy" area, though). There are a few aesthetic differences, but the layout is fairly similar.

As the sermon, or talk, proceeds, you can fill in the blanks that out-line the major topics. The little sheet, handed out beforehand as you enter the sanctuary, makes the whole time a lot easier. If tax deduc-tions — I mean, church donations — are up, they may even distri-bute pens with the name and logo of the church on them. At these churches, the talks are well-structured and center on contemporary issues such as _____, _____, and _____ (like some kind of Christian *MAD LIB™*)

Normally the jokes are better, too.

A song or communion might be next.

Both services end after one more closing prayer, or the occasional circle prayer, and the preacher proceeds to the rear of the church, through the double door, and positions himself in the foyer or nar-thex with a couple of the elders.

(As a side note, I always thought the word "narthex" was way too cool for church. It would be a killer name for a metal band though. Feel free to use it — all I ask for is 10% of gross.)

All who walk out of the church can say their goodbyes and shake hands as they proceed down the stairs and out into the world.

If Only Thou Wilst Believeth
We have been instructed time and time again how trusting, praying and believing are the route to this blessed life of increase — the healthy family, the Christian children, the promotion, even the money for the car when it broke down unexpectedly. People find 20-dollar bills where before there were none. It becomes a trade-off, a give-and-take with God. We get what we want and say, "Well, isn't God good!"

"Isn't life good — praise the Lord! — let's go to church!"

And you are satisfied. As well you should be: the spell worked and you got your reward.

But for the moment, I ask, why has Christianity been reduced to such an "if-then" set of standards aimed at healthy and successful living?

If I think good thoughts, *then* I'll always be healthy.

If I enroll my kids in a Christian school, *then* they won't do drugs.

If I have perfect church attendance, *then* I'll get that promotion.

If I pray before I eat, *then* people will know I am a Christian.

If I pray enough, *then* this city will change.

If I tithe more, *then* I'll be more successful.

If I hand out free drinks, *then* this community will see increase.

If I give the homeless crack addict a ride, *then* I'll get a new car.

If I make fun of retards, *then* my kids will be retarded.

If I _____, *then* _____ (fill in the blanks)

Doesn't this regiment deserve a closer look?

Has it always been this selfishly driven by promises of profit and praise?

When did our faith have more to do with what we get out of it than with what God has put into it? We love Him because of His love for us.

And when you love someone, you're not thinking about what you're getting out of it. You're only concern is pleasing the love of your life.

This improper view of Christianity that treats God as a merchant more than a husband is one of the main reasons there is so much tension in the Church. There are too many "special interest" groups in churches lobbying to reach out to the lost and the unloved and the hated, all for the wrong reasons. Sadly, sometimes they do so only because they think they're "commanded" too, with little or no sincerity involved.

Maybe we would all be better off by questioning things a little bit more.

Think about how this poor standard of market-theology creates an environment where the Church must satisfy the congregation and the unbelievers as well, in order to keep them or pull them in respectively. It's no longer about God's love so much as it's about maintaining the money flow.

All of this is enslaving the gospel to the wishes and wants of a congregation intent on having it their way.

This is a result of marrying our faith to the "have-it-your-way" worldview of modern society. Not only is it okay, but but it is encouraged to place our own happiness above everything else. Our own personal gratification is our priority, and everyone from the makers of our food and clothing all the way up to our elected officials reinforce this belief.

Because they are all making money off of it.

And here's the clincher: so are our churches.

Our churches are making unbelievable amounts of money off of our consumer-oriented approach to "church."

They know that it is no longer about truth.

Rather, a church's existence is only as secure as far as the quality of their children's programs, the modernity of their media equipment, the relevance of their morning worship music, and other cultural conventions can take it.

Haven't we set foot on shifting soil when individuals can snub their noses at the truth and simply pick the church on the next block because they have better things to say, or a better gymnasium?

Don't you think we've taken this consumer selfishness just a little too far in the church today?

Remember When?

When you look back on your life, how did you receive salvation?

For the sake of discussion, I'll assume that it was through a church, while you were in a church, or at some church-organized function like a picnic, Friday-night basketball, city-wide prayer meeting, or Christian-oriented, hardcore music festival.

So more specifically, how were you drawn to your church, initially?

Or how were those you know drawn?

Maybe the following list of surface reasons, with the *"let's get real"* or the *"let's meet people where they really are"* insinuations in italics, will make it easier:

The people at this church are so accepting and loving.

- They don't care if I'm gay/lesbian

They invited me.

- OK, they drugged me

I finally found a preacher I agree with.

- Who doesn't talk about money, money, money

I agree with the people here, their doctrine, that is.

- I can have some wine or a beer with dinner

The people here are great. . .very humble.

- Most of the members are poor

I feel comfortable here.

- No one here has crucifix or angel tattoos

They push me to get out of my comfort zone.

- A couple of the rebels have tattoos of a crucifix or an angel

They have a great children's program or Christian school.

- Where my kids will get a great education based on Christian principles

My family grew up here.

- Before Mom and Dad got divorced

God led me here.

- After what happened at my last church

My (future) girlfriend/boyfriend goes here.

- And he/she isn't waiting till marriage

I love the way they worship!

- They have guitars and drums

I am a _____, so I enjoy going to a _____ church.

- Yeah, just fill in the blanks

I found myself here for awhile, so I just committed to it.

- Not unlike my last ex-girlfriend/ex-boyfriend

They don't sing those old hymns.

- They still sing those old hymns

I can sing at church and people will say it's good

- Even if it sucks

I feel God here.

- Maybe it was just chill bumps, I must have tripped

After going here a while, I was truly blessed!

- Yeah, that $20 I found in my other jeans

They seem to be a Bible-believing church.

- We went through "The Purpose Driven Life"

This church has a great sports program and a really nice gym.

- You know, to pull in the younger kids

I really feel fed at this church.

38

- No really, they have a restaurant adjoined to the building

This church is really close to home and has great parking.

- I can sleep in a little longer on Sunday

I like the Kool-Aid™.

- I like the Kool-Aid™

I acknowledge that there are hundreds more reasons, some valid and some not so valid.

Incidentally, in much of your spiritual reasoning, you will find there is a little too much *you*.

The show is *not* about you.

It is not *your* day or *your* party.

It is not the church's responsibility to make *you* fit in or to make *you* feel happy or successful.

It's not about any of us.

There's Money in the Catering Business

At the current rate of things, the finest churches would become nothing more than social clubs, conveying all that is pleasing (yet still legal, in the Christian sense), attracting the masses for service and converting unbelievers by the power of any of a number of extra-curricular activities.

There will be that church that "caters" to the old folks, the one that loves on the punk rockers, the one for the Jews, the one for the Gentiles, the one that helps people mend their spending habits, the good old-fashioned church that knows things need to be the way they used to be (even though, at one time, they themselves were revolutionary).

And pretty soon, there will be millions of single-member churches.

Their passion plays won't be worth much, but their disagreements will be down by 100%.

Modern churches have this attitude that, by addressing the stereotypes (the successful businessman, the punk rocker, the pastel golfer) and approaching them as such — showing that Christianity is cool if that is what it needs to be or is sporty if that is what it needs to be — then the unsaved can be reached on their own terms with a Christianity that meets people and loves them where they are. Become all things to all people, that by all means some might be saved. Get the people involved and then snatch 'em up for the Lord.

That actually sounds pretty effective at first, and even Biblical.

But look a little closer.

Instead of a God who calls all sorts of people from all walks of life into His church, thus doing away with the punk rocker and the businessman, golfer and couch potato, Jew and Greek, etc., what we really have is nothing short of a falling away. People are leaving the Church (upper-case) and forming their own churches (lower-case). When this happens, they are committing a severe, and damaging, act of discrimination.

The Businessman

Think about this businessman who is at the end of a very long undertaking:

He has achieved his education; he owns his own corporation; he has a perfect wife, perfect kids; he wants nothing.

Now something completely unpredictable happens — grace.

His eyes are opened to how much he actually does lack; he even begins to see himself in a different light; he's not as witty as he thought he was. Instead, he's hurtful and sarcastic; he's not a ladies' man — in fact, he's unfaithful. Neither is he financially well-off, he's actually a swindler and a liar.

Without a doubt, his eyes have been opened.

He sees himself fully for the first time: sin and all.

And he doesn't like what he sees.

He receives faith in Jesus Christ, leading to his salvation; he begins going to church; he finds himself forming deep, loving relationships with people he never thought he would spend five minutes with.

He worships beside a teenager with a Mohawk. On the other side of him is a man who is just getting back on his feet after being homeless for ten years.

In fact, everyone in the church is so different from himself, but somehow, he loves all of them, and they all love him. The businessman finds that he has left his prejudices at the door of his old life.

The Young Hipster
That's one take on things. But now think about this girl — twenty-eight years old and an emotional martyr for the case of Christ:

She starts attending church.

She soon finds herself very critical of the music.

She thinks, "This isn't going to reach my friends."

"My friends would think this is incredibly cheesy."

She wants hardcore music; she wants to see kids in leather jackets; she wants to see kids in spiked boots come to Jesus.

She leaves the church and starts her own.

She focuses on her peers.

She makes Jesus fashionable for her rock-and-roll contemporaries.

Although on surface-level what this girl has done appears to be loaded with zeal and good-will, rooted in a desire to reach those she loves, she has, in effect, severed the businessman mentioned first from ever being a part of her community.

Feeling culturally excluded herself, she did not seek to tear down any barriers that she may have seen which would have kept her from a fuller relationship with her former brothers and sisters in Christ.

Instead, she placed culture and surface-level appearances over the meaning of Church as a community of believers who have been *called out* of all sorts of walks of life.

It's no longer about Jesus Christ. It's about appealing to a certain stereotype. And even if it's from a positive vantage point, it's still wrong. And we find ourselves right back at consumer-controlled Christianity.

What will happen when a culture at which the gospel has been aimed begins to conflict with the truth?

Which will be compromised?

Too often, it is the gospel that takes a back seat.

So, What's Jesus Wearing Today?

You can't put Jesus in leather pants. Decking Him out in "relevant" threads does not make him any more accessible to the masses.

You can't put him in a suit.

He's not a CEO.

He's not a bum.

He's not just concerned with starving children in Africa.

Nor is He only after "the terrorists."

The prognosis?

Nothing more than pious pimps prostituting cheap imitations to the promiscuous masses — turning tricks to turn a dollar.

When we get caught up in forcing Jesus into our cultural and political schemes, we place those cultures and schemes above the cross.

Is that how we want to do business?

The Chemical Resistancy
of the Masses

A good friend of mine humorously relates to me an anecdote he calls:

THE CHEMICAL SALESMAN
MODEL OF CHRISTIANITY

And the chemical is, you guessed it, Christianity.

Like a precisely-placed intravenous needle, it permeates into your veins and muscles and begins to direct your actions and motives. Introduction to this chemical is TOXIC!

If you become saturated with the chemical to a certain point - that is, if exposed hard enough and long enough - you cannot help but become a Christian.

Our job as sanctified Christians then, is to basically act as pharmaceutical reps or chemical sales people in order to deliver as much chemical to as many future proponents of Christianity as possible.

This task is accomplished through a myriad of functions: for many, it is church fellowship and community friendship; for others, it may be a church basketball team or other extra-curricular activities; for still others, it may be through that damned rock music (that still has a Christian message, of course).

If, indeed, we are licensed Chemical Salesmen to begin with, then it is our work and our service to labor after this task for however long it may require to infuse the unbeliever with enough chemical agent so that saturation is complete.

Then they might believe.

Then they will be saved.

The unfortunate part of the entire matter is that some people seem resistant to the chemical. No matter how much they are exposed, they find Jesus just as repugnant as before.

For some it is a strong aversion — the mere sight of the chemical invokes a vomitous rejection.

For others, it may be that they can withstand the chemical for a time and then they either succumb or revolt.

For still others, they may seem to have surrendered to the chemical's influence and then later relapsed into immunity or even repulsion.

Herein lies the disconnect.

The problem is that, though the chemical is perfectly sufficient to breed believers, we sales people are completely insufficient for the task of delivering it and creating believers.

It could even be said that we have no presence in the equation at all.

I could see the slogan on some midnight TV add:

"Don't throw your money away on imitations — this stuff really works!"

"It literally sells itself!"

Indeed, unbelievers become believers under many different circumstances — sometimes we Christians happen to be around, but not in every instance.

However, they **always** become believers when they are exposed to the True Chemical and come to know the True Chemical Salesman, or rather, when they come to be known by Him.

Salvation is a work of God that is perfect and everlasting.

When you look back and ask yourself,

"Why am I saved and how did I come to be interested in the things of God?"

Wouldn't it be reassuring to know that it rested in His enduring strength and not your own?

In His persistent might and not that of some humanistic philosophy or psychology?

Christianity doesn't need molded to find you where you are.

It would then prove to be an impostor religion.

The counterfeit results that spring up when salvation comes from our hands are embarrassing to Christianity, and are another cause of much of what we see today.

Those Stupid Church Books *Next* to the Bibles

It is important to realize that the stupidity of Christian books is not confined only to the Christian fiction and Christian living sections.

Possibly the largest section in the bookstore, incidentally, is the Bibles section.

In fact, if you put enough different versions of *The Message*, *The Message Remix*, *The Message Strikes Back*, and *Return of the Message* on a single shelf, you begin to see the wood sweat at the overbearing weight of it all. Even Atlas may shrug.

I appreciate just about any good English translation as much as the next guy.

Nevertheless, countless people have interpreted Scripture countless ways and integrated it right into their very own "version" of the Bible.

Let's take a quick peek — or maybe a long stare — at the number of English versions floating around out there:

American Standard Version (ASV)
American King James Version (AKJV)
Amplified Bible (AMP)
An American Translation
Analytical-Literal Translation (ALT)
ArtScroll
Berkeley Version
Bible in Basic English
The Bible in Living English
Bishops' Bible
Children's King James Version
Christian Community Bible
Clear Word Bible
Complete Jewish Bible
Contemporary English Version (CEV)
A Conservative Version
Darby Bible
Douay-Rheims Bible
EasyEnglish Bible
Easy-to-Read Version
English Jubilee 2000 Bible
English Standard Version (ESV)
Ferrar Fenton Bible
Geneva Bible
God's Word
Good News Translation (GNT)
Great Bible
Green's Literal Translation (GLT)
Holmann Christian Standard Bible (HCSB)
Jerusalem Bible
Jewish Publication Society of America Version (JPSAV)
Judaica Press
Julia E. Smith Parker Translation

King James 2000 Version (2KJV)
King James Version (KJV)
Knox's Translation of the Vulgate
Lamsa Bible
Leeser Bible
The Living Bible
The Living Torah and the Living Nach

The Message
Matthew Bible
Modern King James Version (MKJV)
Modern Language Version
Moffatt, New Translation
James Murdock's Translation of the Syriac Peshitta
New American Bible (NAB)
New American Standard Bible (NASB)
New Century Version (NCV)
New English Bible (NEB)
New English Translation (NET)
New International Reader's Version (NIRV)
New International Version Inclusive Language Edition (NIVI)
New International Version (NIV)
New Jerusalem Bible (NJB)
New Jewish Publication Society of America Version
New King James Version (NKJV)
New Life Version (NLV)
New Living Translation (NLT)
New Revised Standard Version (NRSV)
New World Translation of the Holy Scriptures (NWT)
Quaker Bible
Recovery Version of the Bible
Restored Name King James Version
Revised Version
Revised Standard Version (RSV)
Revised Standard Version Catholic Edition (RSVC)
Revised English Bible (REB)
Rotherham's Empahsized Bible
Simplified English Bible
The Story Bible
Taverner's Bible
Thomson's Translations

Today's New International Version (TNIV)
Third Millennium Bible
Tyndale Bible
Updated King James Version (UpKJV)
A Voice In The Wilderness Holy Scriptures
Webster's Revision
Westminster Bible
Wyclif's Bible
Young's Literal Translation (YLT)

Quite a list, isn't it?

For anyone who can read the comics, there should be at least one out of the 82 Bibles listed above that present the Word in a way that you can understand it.

The Inspired Gnostic Nerd

And in addition to the Bibles themselves, and as an added aid in understanding, there is almost always, in Christian circles, that one individual who displays a hermeneutical prowess during the house group sessions that most people mistakenly view as inspired intelligence. More often than not, however, it's merely artificial intelligence. But certainly this leader could help the uninformed.

People like this remind me of modern *Gnostics*, though. Gnostics were an early group of "mystics," who latched on to Christianity fairly quickly, and began talking about getting to God through this "secret knowledge" (doesn't sound much different than what folks are still saying today, does it?).

But you'll find at least one person like this in every Christian group. They have spent more time learning Greek terms and biblical contexts, so they lord it over the "uninitiated," thus elevating themselves to a higher place in their circles.

The Inspired Anointed Nerds

In other Christian circles, the Bible has been made out as such an enigmatic text that intelligence and logic alone will not afford the reader any amount of comprehension.

For these circles, the blessed few who will have the anointing, perhaps the pastors or elders, will teach the ignorant remnant.

These anointed few represent the scriptural filter that delivers comprehension to the masses in a way that the Bible was unable to deliver.

This filter often reveals itself as some "secret," that until now, was hidden from Christianity's view or something that Christianity has forgotten.

These people pretend to hold some higher form of mysticism through feeling and emotion, as if their intuitions were better guides than the Bible itself.

The Republic Community of Inspired Nerds

In still other Christian circles, a divine inspiration imparted from above has allowed the full understanding of Scripture by every single church member, allowing prophecy to spew from the mouth of every believer.

The Grand Admiral of the Republic Community of Inspired Nerds (who asked to remain anonymous) relayed to me the following tool of Christian Divination one day after house group. He warned it should only be used in the most dire of circumstances.

I have since come to call this method of Christian soothsaying the "Holy Flip."

THE HOLY FLIP

For the sake of illustration, lets say Jake (or Max, or some other analogy-efficient, seeker-sensitive, casually-relevant named Christ-follower) is considering taking a new job offer as a barista at the Church cafe.

He really needs this job. But he doesn't know if God is calling him here or not.

So where does he turn?

You guessed it, the Holy Flip.

What is this Holy Flip?

Well, it's simple, really.

Anyone who's handled the well-known Magic 8-Ball will be familiar with the inner workings of this tool of Christian mystics.

But where the 8-Ball fails in its ambiguity, providing the fortune teller with only vague answers such as *yes, no,* or *maybe,* the Bible, through the power of the Holy Flip, is able to provide the fortune teller. . .er, uh. . . seeking prophetic Christian. . .with the efficiency and accuracy that is due any respected diviner.

This is similar to the notion implied by the statement: "if I stop at this red-light, then God saved me from a wreck that was going to happen if I had ran the light. . ."

To use the Holy Flip, Jake simply grabs his *Message and the Temple of Doom* Bible, asks a question, and, you got it, *flips!*

In the act of flipping the Bible open, Jake transforms the Holy Scriptures into his own personal, Western version of the I Ching.

Here is what he does:

Develop question
Should I take this new job?

Initiate the flip
fliiiiiiiiiiiip. . .and. . .no whammy. . .and. . .stop!

Receive answer
"For if ye do this thing indeed, then shall there enter in by the gates of this house kings sitting upon the throne of David, riding in chariots and on horses, he, and his servants, and his people."

Interpret
He thinks this means yes. And a new car!

You get the point.

Deviation, Manipulation, and Other Fancy Terms that End in *-ation*

At first glance, the notions of mystery and secrecy in the previous chapter could easily be applied to a myriad of different religion-based groups.

How often did the medieval Catholic Church horde power over the masses with the use of superior intelligence?

But on the other hand, how often is power controlled with emotion in the multitudes of today's mainstream Protestant denominations?

It's no longer intelligence that hinders the masses from seeing the light.

It is feel-good-ism.

The neglect of the gospel is overlooked by believers because, well, the pastor makes them feel good. Sure, he or she may not always be preaching or living in a way that reflects the gospel of Jesus, but their sermons make everyone feel so darn good about themselves.

And they quote the Bible all the time, so it can't be all bad, can it?

Can it?

The prosperity Gospel is alive and well.

Worry not about how God cares about the poor and oppressed, the widows and the orphans. Worry rather about that new Porsche you just sowed a seed for through that television ministry you love so much.

Worry not about the fact that God's people "did without" for centuries, and the apostles had next to nothing, and that the favor of God did not always, in Scripture, mean financial or physical well-being. Worry rather about how God cares about your financial status, and wants *you* to be filthy rich. It is your destiny.

The American masses are devouring this stuff in record numbers.

Upon closer inspection though, this error of emotion trumping knowledge can be shown to be one of the biggest tell-tale signs of just about every cult in existence!

Why then are we, as a Church, allowing emotionalism to trump the gospel in our communities?

When defending the faith against these out-groups, it is easy to claim in defense of traditional Christianity that one must rely *solely* on Scripture.

But are we sipping the same Kool-Aid™ that the cults are?

Consider the examples set forth by Mary Baker Eddy, "mother" of Christian Science, or by Charles Taze Russell, founder of the Jehovah's Witnesses, as quoted from Walter R. Martin's *Kingdom of the Cults*. In the *Christian Science Journal* (pages 116 and 117), January 1901, Mrs. Eddy points out how divine knowledge brought her such understanding of the Word:

> I should blush to write of the *Science and Health, With Key to the Scriptures* as I have, were it of human origin and I apart from God its author, but as I was only a scribe echoing the harmonies of heaven in divine metaphysics, I cannot be super-modest of the Christian Science textbook.

Perhaps hovering somewhere past the notion of sacred tradition, the following statement concerning Christian Science was discovered in a personal letter to Mrs. Eddy's friend in 1877 (page 117, from *The Life of Mary Baker G. Eddy*, George I. Milmine, page 73):

> "The idea given by God this time is higher, clearer and more permanent than before."

The Jehovah's Witnesses also seem to partake of the same mystic Kool-Aid™.

In the September 15, 1910 edition of the *The Watch Tower*, page 298, "Pastor" Russell makes the following statement concerning his "Studies in the Scriptures" and their "indispensable" value when examining the Bible (page 41, emphasis belongs to Martin):

> If the six volumes of "Scripture Studies" are practically the Bible, topically arranged with Bible proof texts given, we might not improperly name the volumes "The Bible in an Arranged Form." That is to say, they are not mere comments on the Bible, but *they are practically the Bible* itself. Furthermore, not only do we find that *people cannot see the divine plan in studying the Bible by itself,* but we see, also, that if anyone lays the "Scriptures Studies" aside, even after he has used them, after he has become familiar with them, after he has read them for ten years — if he then lays them aside and ignores them and goes to the Bible alone, though he has understood his Bible for ten years, our experience shows that within two years *he goes into darkness.* On the other hand, if he had merely read the "Scripture Studies" with their references and *had not read a page of the Bible as such,* he would be in the *light* at the end of the two years because he would have the light of the Scriptures.

Deviation and manipulation are terms normally and most easily applied to the activities of cultic groups, but might they also be applied closer to home? Or is the Kool-Aid too sweet for you?

[NOTE: The remaining paragraphs are best read in a Cajun accent. For example: deviaSHAWN, manipulaSHAWN, etc., etc.]

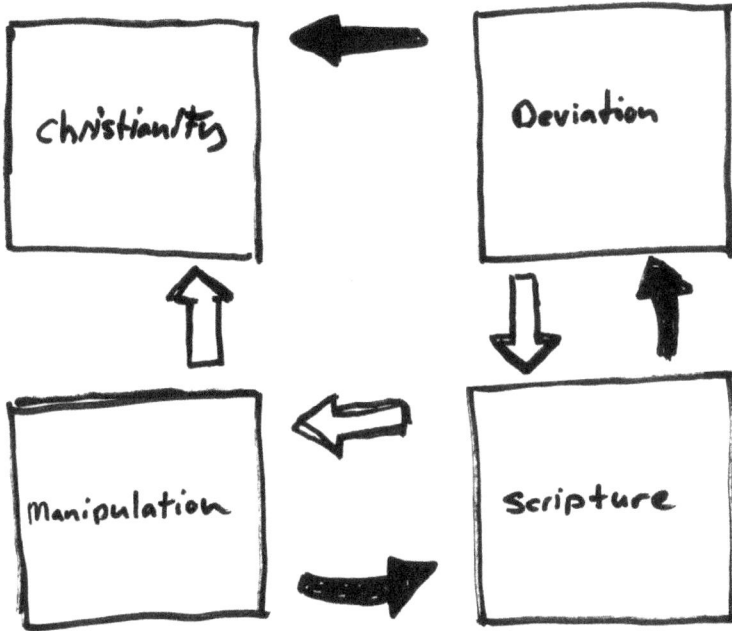

Deviation

Deviation from Scripture is often one of the first and most apparent signs of a group's manipulation of Christianity.

Deviation, or departing, from Scripture could demonstrate itself in a number of ways: certain teachings and traditions or synergistic views of salvation. When the Bible is diminished, and its trustworthiness as a spiritual authority is downplayed, the formula for a cult is created.

All cults have to figure out what to do with the Bible.

Manipulation *of* the faith begins with deviation *from* the Bible.

Manipulation

Likewise, *manipulation* of Scripture is often one of the first, and most apparent, signs of a group's deviation from Christianity.

Manipulation *of* Scripture is probably slightly more intentional than deviation *from* Scripture, but hopefully more easily identifiable: partial quotes, twisted theologies, and various mal-intentioned schemes.

Although sometimes more obvious than a complete deviation from the Bible, manipulation can be more dangerous, because it still contains the shell of truth. It uses the same terminology.

It's like putting dog crap in a candy bar wrapper: it might very well look sweet, but you're in for a BIG surprise when you take that first bite.

These steps away from genuine Christianity, are not always so readily identifiable, but are often at the heart of many movements such as the New Age Movement, Post-Modernism, and the Emergent Church.

The Classy Cuisine Model

It's been said that after the $25.00 steak meal, everything more expensive is based on additional quality, not quantity. Incidentally, the quality of such classy cuisines rarely relies on taste alone.

Often the presentation is the money shot; the uniqueness and pleasure rest equally in layout and appearance rather than solely on substance.

The Christian market, whether it be books, music, or church itself, is not unlike ordering a classy cuisine. Sometimes you're just paying for the pomp.

But look specifically at the Bible market in American Christianity.

Bible translation is (or should be) tough work — the result of comprehensive language study, prayer, attention to detail, and many, many hours of tedious examination.

Fortunately though, for today's Christian writers anyways, there exists a new paradigm of financially successful authorship.

Capitalizing on the Word that was already written, it seems that out-lining, organizing, adding pictures, stories, or study helps, or simply re-shaping, have proved very profitable.

Having seen the "meat" (the Bible versions) let's now examine the presentation (kinds of Bibles). Here we can see a sampling of various kinds of Bibles I have crossed paths with at bookstores or online:

Audio	Moms-to-Be
Bilingual	Multi-Cultural
Bride's	New Testament
Catholic	One Year
Charismatic	Parallel
Children's	Pastoral Interest
Chronological	Pentecostal
Compact & Pocket	Pew
Devotional	Pulpit
Duct-Tape	Reference
Economy & Ministry	Slimline
Family	Software
Gift & Award	Soldier's
Golfer's	Student
Graduate	Study
Groom's	Teens
Heirloom	Thinline
Interlinear	Topical
Large/Giant Print	Tropical
Lectern	Ultrathin
Lego-based	Visual
Life Application	Wedding

I am not sure what is more amazing: that there are so many different versions and kinds or that Christians financially support such endeavors. People fall for it every day.

Perhaps *ludicrous* is the word we're searching for, here.

How far will these authors go to scratch the itching ears?

Too far.

Consider the following Bible titles available:

Ray Comfort
- *The Evidence Bible: Irrefutable Evidence for the Thinking Mind, Comfort-able King James Version*

Jack Hayford
- *The New Spirit Filled Life Bible* (NKJV)

Jack Van Impe
- *Jack Van Impe Prophecy Bible*

T.D. Jakes
- *The Holy Bible, Woman Thou Art Loosed! Edition*

Max Lucado
- *Children's Daily Devotional Bible*
- *The Devotional Bible: Experience the Heart of Jesus*
- *The Grace for the Moment Daily Bible: Spend 365 Days reading the Bible with Max Lucado*
- *He Did This Just For You New Testament With Reflections From Max Lucado*
- *The Inspirational Bible, The Everyday Bible*
- *Max Lucado's Hermie and Friends Bible*

John C. Maxwell
- *The Maxwell Leadership Bible: Lessons in Leadership from the Word of God*

Joyce Meyer
- *The Everyday Life Bible: The Power of God's Word for Everyday Living*

Thomas Nelson
- *Compact Kids Bible: Grasshopper Glittergreen*
- *The Duct Tape Bible*
- *My First Catholic Bible For Catholic Children Who Want A Devotional Bible Of Their Very Own!*
- *New Spirit-Filled Life Bible: Kingdom Equipping Through the Power of the Word*

Eugene H. Peterson
- *The Daily Message*
- *The Message: The Bible in Contemporary Language*
- *The Message Remix*
- *The Message Remix 2.0*

Charles Stanley
- *The Charles F. Stanley Life Principles Bible*

Rod Parsley
- *The Bridge Builder's Bible*

A Fine Meal from the Depths of eBay

I particularly liked that last one. On February 29, 2008, with $18.35, plus $3.99 shipping and handling, you could have had the winning bid on this beauty at eBay (photo from eBay):

A signed copy of the *Bridge Builder's Bible*! Featuring the autograph of — none other than — Rod Parsley!

At only 18 bucks, I thought it was a steal.

Though the book was used, the seller did have a 99.9% positive feedback. He had this to say about his item (emphasis belongs to eBay seller):

> I AM OFFERING, BRIDGE BUILDER'S BIBLE, ROD PARSLEY 10 GOLDEN KEYS SPECIAL EDITION. THIS IS THE KING JAMES VERSION, CONCORDANCE, MAPS, RED LETTER EDITION. IT IS SIGNED BY ROD PARSLEY. IT IS THE ENTIRE BIBLE. THE COLOR IS BURGUNDY. I FOUND NO MARKINGS IN THE TEXT AND NO FORMER OWNER'S NAMES IN THE BOOK, EXCEPT OF COURSE ROD PARSLEYS' SIGNATURE. GENESIS THROUGH REVELATION. THE 1997 EDITION IS IN VERY GOOD PLUS

> CONDITION. THE COVERS AND SPINE ARE
> FLAWLESS!! THERE IS SOME WEAR ON THE
> BOTTOM OUTSIDE FACE GOLD PAGES,
> WHERE THERE IS FADING. IT LOOKS AND
> FEELS LIKE LEATHER. THE SIZE IS 6 1/4 BY 9
> 1/4 INCHES. I ACCEPT PAYPAL, MONEY
> ORDER AND CHECK. COMBINE AUCTIONS
> AND SAVE ON SHIPPING!!

Surprisingly, or not surprisingly, there is even a *Hooked On Phonics* Bible — works for me!

Opportunity knocks for these authors, and they, without hesitation, never fail to answer.

Bon Appetit! Enjoy your meal.

Rise of
the Religitards

Back in the Christian Living Section, I find myself actually biting my tongue or suppressing laughter as I read the various titles or view the eye-catching covers of the numerous Stupid Church Books. If these were music albums, some Matt Redman would have written a Heart of Worship song, an "I'm sorry Lord for the thing I made it" song, well before now.

Even veteran-Stupid-Church-Book-Author and now-proclaimed American Christian Leader, Rick Warren, noticed this when he quoted the lyrics to that very song in *The Purpose-Driven Life*. Nevertheless, these new books keep popping up every day.

You have books dealing with financial affairs all the way down to what to feed your dog.

Christians feel they need the information in such books, but feel better, maybe more "Christian," to purchase the work of a Christian author — someone they can trust.

A good friend of mine (a truly genuine Christian, but one who probably would not agree with the title of my book) notes that these books are using Christian principles to combat secular problems. If he is going to seek out financial solutions or the like, then he would at least feel better getting information with a Christian slant, supporting a Christian author rather than gathering vain philosophies, supporting secular entities.

But perhaps these Christian authors merely gathered those vain philosophies, threw a cross on their findings, and sold it at a higher price.

And it makes you wonder: maybe Christians buy such titles because they feel the knowledge held within them is necessary for that extra hint of joy in life. Like maybe life won't be so good unless they buy a certain book, and obtain the information found therein. Sadly, that's the attitude that people sell these books on.

A fear-based form of marketing that says:

"*If* you don't buy A, *then* you'll lack B."

Incidentally, if I were to understand Christianity by the topics presented in the Christian Living section, I would have to admit that Christians must be some of the more needy, downtrodden, depressed and otherwise unsuccessful individuals in all of God's creation.

Women need loosing, driving needs purpose, and everyone's life seems to need "bettering" or "besting."

Apart from the subject matter presented within these books, is the nature of true Christianity accurately represented by these titles, or do these titles represent a pseudo-Christianity, one full of consumers eager to purchase the next bestseller that will yield them fresh victory?

Even worse, is it possible that these titles encourage a weakened Christianity?

Are these titles selling because people cannot do without the wisdom, or are there other reasons, like a killer marketing strategy that we mentioned earlier?

Upon examination of Amazon's Christian Living Bestseller list, it is evident there are several conventions that most authors adhere to. Somewhere, maybe in the basement of some famous publisher, there must be a course that authors attend concerning the rationale for successful Church Book endeavors. (By the way, a similar course, in that same basement, is attended by Christian musicians before they create, name, and brand their bands. If it hasn't been written yet, there is probably a large market for a book on the subject: I only ask for a 10% commission.)

For those of you who do not have the privilege of attending the course and because we haven't yet found the book on it, the following chapter will guide you through the process of hyping your next Stupid Church Book.

Let's Make
a Deal!

The most successful authors realize that the entire life of their career hinges on applying the five principles of Stupid Church Book Hype.

The principles are so intertwined that it is hard to fully define their boundaries and even their sequence. If I were a better Stupid Church Book author, I would have found words that made a memorable little pneumonic, like C.R.O.S.S., or F.A.I.T.H., but instead we are left with S.T.C.M.F.:

Story, Title, Cover, Marketing and Follow-up.

Being among the ranks of Stupid Church Books, I suppose it is fitting that many of the topics held herein might originate from talks and times at a bookstore.

Whenever I go to the bookstore, it's a childlike joy for me to jaunt down the "Christian" and "Christian Living" aisles. For me, it's a humorous field trip into religiously ludicrous territory. Sometimes, though, when there are other shoppers nearby, searching for the new Dekker, Olsteen, or Meyer titles, I feel a certain amount of sorrow and anger: sorrow for the customer, and anger for the advertising and marketing folks who do such a grand job of snaring people in and making them think that they *need* that book on the shelf.

Here's what I see happening:

Some type of market springs up or becomes popular on Tuesday and a hundred enterprising types latch on by Wednesday. Be it books in general, or Christian fiction alone, or Contemporary Christian music, or even Christian motorcycle gangs, soccer leagues, schools, or positive and successful thinking seminars. At least by the weekend, a million bottom feeders devour the new meat, hungry for more by Monday morning.

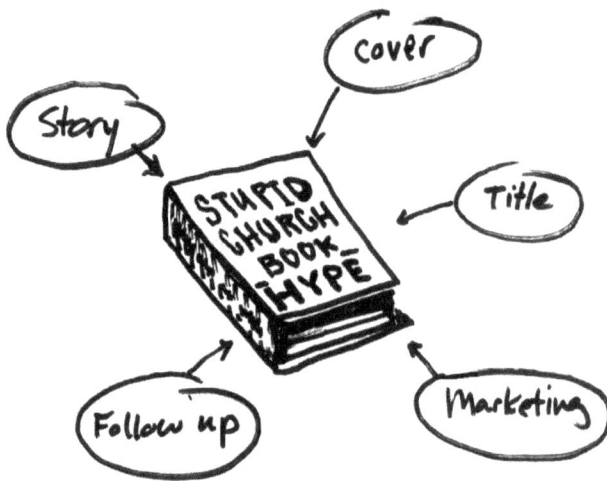

I wonder if Paul's tent-making business had a cheesy sign out front reminding all that "God is my Co-seamstress," or perhaps the company name was A-Tent-ive to Christ or Trinity Tents and Knots (remember, he was a forward-thinking revolutionary, so maybe he was pushing the envelope with this "Trinity" thing). Do you think that there would have been an ictus below the phone number on his sign?

STUPID CHURCH BOOK HYPE: STORY

Recently at the bookstore, my interests were truly piqued when I saw one particular cover:

23 Minutes in Hell by Bill Wiese.

That's right.

Just like Lazarus, this gentleman (a real-estate agent) retells his account and provides a stern warning after he descended into hell for nearly half an hour.

Come to find out, hell is quite uncomfortable.

It has prison cells with bars, if you can believe it, and well, alright — I'll give the guy one thing: at least the he *does* claim that hell is real.

Let's examine this through Josh McDowell's line of reasoning:

The Lord Possibility

The guy went to hell, God pulled him out, he tells the world through his book, and some are saved.

The Liar Possibility

The guy had this ingenious plan to write a book about hell, God allows it to publish and sell, the world hears about it, and some are saved.

The Lunatic Possibility

The guy thinks he went to hell, he somehow manages to write and publish a book, the world hears about it, and some are saved.

All of these possibilities promote people's salvation.

The synergist might say that they help "save" people.

All of these could possibly be defended by Scripture.

All of these put money in the author's pocket.

So what is the basis of your salvation?

Maybe you are still struggling and need some confirmation. I guess I might have been a skeptic, too, if I hadn't had a similar experience.

11:23

It was an uncommonly frigid morning – one of the last days of autumn. I strapped up my hiking boots over my warmest pair of wool socks, zipped up my jacket up to my neck, and proceeded into the forest with hopes of enjoying one last excursion before the snows of winter bound me to the reading room. I had only planned on walking a few miles out and a few miles back but my wife still reminded me to take my water bottle in case I got thirsty along the way. She had bought us matching sport bottles with each other s names on them.

Without a doubt, the scenery in West Virginia is unmatched. Though I have seen the same views year after year, I must admit that I am impressed and refreshed anew upon each journey.

I started down my favorite trail, a windy little path that traces the creek s edge – grassy on the flatter sections, rocky and steep where the water cascades over breaks in the bed rock. A couple miles from the trail head, just as the path begins to narrow and brings you through thick undergrowth and compromising terrain, one turn in the trail reveals a small bridge. Crossing the bridge you gain your first glimpse of an entire vista blanketed by knee-high grass, swaying in the breeze. The field goes on for miles and miles. It is one of those views that make you wish you had your camera only to realize that if you did, you still wouldn t be able to capture the magnitude of what lay stretched in front of you.

This view alone was often the purpose of my trip.

I was making good time today - it was only 9:00am - so I decided to continue along a new trail that I had never seen before, just beyond the bridge.

This decision will be with me for the rest of my life.

+ + +

I knew where I was.

At least I thought I did.

I still felt dizzy and wasn t quite sure what had just happened.

I was curious why it was already getting dark out.

Then, fuzzy recollections slowly pieced the story together as I faded in and out of consciousness.

I had to be on that new trail - by a waterfall but off to the side in the rocks.

I heard something behind me in the brush.

It was so hot, so smokey.

I must have passed out.

I fell. . .no. . .worse.

Something had fell on me. . .no, something has attacked me!

I rolled forward to find my legs in shrouds.

They were ravaged as if some hungry animal had ripped into my flesh for meat.

I reached forward to examine the damage. . .but felt nothing.

I literally felt nothing.

I squinted, peering through my blood-caked eyelashes.

Double take.

My arm lay several feet in front of me at the end of a trail of blood.

Upon realization of the state I was in, excruciating pain races through my body – what is left of it.

Fervent flames and engulfing smoke now encircled my position.

I lift my head to see two dark figures hovering over my body as one gouges some part of its form into my abdomen and extracts my innards out into the open air.

My head rolls back and my eyes shut, but the pain, it still remains; the heat, it still remains.

All I can utter is "save me."

The voice thundered louder than anything I had ever heard:

"DEPART!"

The figures scream in terror as the darkness is transformed.

I hear shrieking and thrashing and wailing.

With my eyes clinched shut I can tell the sky is aglow, brighter than the sun.

A mighty rushing wind sweeps over the rocks.

It grows stronger until I feel it lifts my body from the surface.

I am floating now.

The pain recedes from my body and then silence.

Absolute silence.

It is broken by a single whispered word breathed out near my ear:

"Peace."

+ + +

Again, I lay on the ground. Already I can feel it is softer. A light breeze begins to blow and I hear the rustling of tall grass all around me.

"No pain," I think to myself.

I open my eyes anticipating what may await me in my sight. It is the field! I slowly transition my eyes down to my body.

I am complete!

My legs, they are healed!

My arm, it is attached!

There is no blood; my clothes - they are totally fresh.

I must have lay there for couple of hours contemplating what had just happened - why had it happened. Did it really happen? Finally, I stood. I walked back through the grass until I found familiar territory and began to head back home. Just before I crossed the bridge, I looked to the left and noticed a sign for a new trail. Was this here earlier? I had to see where it went. I decided I would check it out.

I checked my watch: 11:23am.

I will give it at least a few minutes, tops. The trail took me along another creek. It did feel familiar, but I get that feeling in a lot of places.

Then I saw the waterfall.

An eerie chill creeps down the middle of my back. I thought that was a dream. . .Now, cautious in my steps, I continued closer where an outcropping of rocks hid a small cove. Lodged between two of the rocks I spotted a melted mass of plastic. I leaned over to examine it. As I picked it up I noticed it was very warm. My jaw dropped in amazement and paralyzing chills raced up and down my spine. I could make out letters along the underside, still intact:

"Nadya s Man."

It was my water bottle!

I ran the whole way home, never losing a breath. It hadn t sunk in yet. I knew it happened, but what had just happened.

Why had it happened? My life was changed. I experienced such a spiritual renewal.

It took at least a couple months to understand that day.

It took a couple years to research it Biblically and write the next Christian Living best-seller.

Who am I: Lord? Liar? or Lunatic?

Perhaps you can't accept this as truth.

Actually, you shouldn't accept this as truth (yeah, maybe I am the Liar!); occasionally I like to try my hand at fiction. But this type of exchange is the substance of today's life-changing experiences.

This is the stuff books are made of — seriously.

People need these stories and events to know the supernatural is very natural.

Now this particular story may have been a little C.S. Lewis-y, but it could just as easily have been about pain and suffering during a mission trip at the hands of savage cannibals or during street ministry at the hands of angry homeless people. It could even have been a little less bloody and set at work or home.

Just remember, charlatans everywhere are becoming all things to all people, that by all means, though some might be "saved," all might give a few bucks to help out the charlatan business.

The account of *11:23* doesn't add a single ounce of credibility to the reality that is Christianity.

The reality is already complete.

STUPID CHURCH BOOK HYPE: TITLE

The largest part of the Christian aisle is probably the how-to section — the self-help section.

I wonder why it is called "self-help" when reading an author's book is evidence enough that the reader can't handle it on his own?

Perhaps it should be called the Stupid-Church-Book-Author-Help Section.

Anyways, for any of a number of issues there is a solution. It is probably only a matter of following several steps.

One popular technique is the numbers game. Give your readers a number of steps or a number of ways to do something or handle something. I did notice that this was the case with numerous titles. It seems that, in the Christian market, we all *love* a good set of numbers. We don't want to fool with the messy part of life, with all its sin and disorganization and chaos.

Just give us a few books with lists on how to take care of our problems.

That's all we need.

Here are a few, starting from the top:

- *189 Ways to Contact God* by Marlene Halpin
- *101 Ways to Reach Your Community* by Steve Sjogren
- *50 Ways to Pray: Practices from Many Traditions and Times* by Teresa Blythe
- *44 Steps Up Off the Plateau* by Lyle E. Schaller
- *Hearing God: 30 Different Ways* by Larry Kreider
- *25 Ways to Win with People: How to Make Other Feel Like a Million Bucks* by John C. Maxwell and Les Parrott
- *Our 24 Family Ways: Family Devotional Guide* by Clay Clarkson
- *21 Ways to Finding Peace and Happiness: Overcoming Anxiety, Fear, and Discontentment Every Day* by Joyce Meyer
- *Twenty Steps to Wisdom* by Jennifer James
- *Seventeen Steps to Heaven* by Leo J. Trese
- *And the Angels Held Their Breath: Sixteen Reasons for Exploring the God-Option* by Elaine Farmer
- *Fifteen Secrets for Life and Ministry* by Robert R. Kopp
- *Total Life Prosperity 14 Practical Steps to Receiving God's Full Blessing* by Creflo A. Dollar (perfect name, huh?)
- *The Anger Workbook: A 13-Step Interactive Plan to Help You* by Les Carter and Frank Minirth
- *Twelve Steps to a New Day* by Ron Keller
- *Go Big With Small Groups: Eleven Steps to an Explosive Small Group Ministry* by Bill Easum and John Atkinson
- *10 Steps to Fulfilling Your Divine Destiny: A Christian Woman's Guide to Learning & Living God's Plan for Her* by Marnie L. Pehrson

- *9 Steps for Reversing or Preventing Cancer* by Shivani Goodman, Jack Canfield, and O. Carl Simonton (Christian medical advice, priceless. . .)
- *8 Steps to Create the Life You Want: The Anatomy of a Successful Life* by Creflo A. Dollar (Christian anatomy lessons, even better.)
- *7 Steps to Becoming Financially Free: A Catholic Guide to Managing Your Money* by Phil Lenahan (I'd suggest the Jewish guide!)
- *Six Steps to Spiritual Revival: God's Awesome Power in Your Life* by Pat Robertson
- *5 Steps to Successful Selling* by Zig Ziglar
- *Four Steps to Spiritual Freedom* by Thomas Ryan
- *Three Steps in Defeating Temptation: Insights from James 4:7* by Lyle Dukes
- *The First Step Bible* by Mack Thomas and Joe Stites
- *One Step Closer: Why U2 Matters to Those Seeking God* by Christian Scharen
- *A Tiny Step Away From Deepest Faith: A Teenager's Search For Meaning* by Marjorie Corbman

Two turtle doves and a partridge in a pear tree. . .

It's really not even necessary to add the steps — just throwing a number out there in the mix goes a long way. Take a look at these titles:

- *The 2-degree Difference: How Little Things Can Change Everything* by John Trent
- *3:16: The Numbers of Hope* by Max Lucado
- *9 to 5 Window* by Os Hillman
- *Six Great Ideas* by Mortimer J. Adler
- *Five for Sorrow, Ten for Joy* by Rumer Godden and Joan Chitister

Building on the previous techniques, many authors have successfully combined numbers and times to create the following titles:

- *3 Seconds: The Power of Thinking Twice* by Les Parrott (perhaps he is qualified to repeat things.)
- *One Minute After You Die* by Erwin Lutzer
- *23 Minutes in Hell* by Bill Wiese (see note on 90 Minutes in Heaven, below)
- *90 Minutes in Heaven* by Don Piper (interesting huh? God sent someone to Heaven and Hell and they both wrote books right here around the same time. I wonder if 23 Minutes in Hell would have been so popular had 90 Minutes in Heaven proved a fluke?)
- *Six Hours One Friday* by Max Lucado

Another popular technique is to capitalize on the Christian Couples Market.

These titles fall under the counseling genre, normally tackling his/hers relationship issues like dating and not dating, marriage and divorce, or sex and abstinence.

Part of their success stems from the fact that sex has tended to always be somewhat taboo for Christians to talk about, much less enjoy, even as late as ten to fifteen years ago.

Even now, the issue seems to be overly hushed.

As you will see, however, most of the proceeds are split between two authors; fortunately, those two authors are mostly under the same roof.

So, cuddle up with your better half, tell your secret, and get published.

You might have the next bestseller in the Christian Living Section!

Here are just a few:

- *Men are Like Waffles, Women are Like Spaghetti: Understanding and Delighting in Your Differences* by Bill Farrel and Pam Farrel
- *Moments Together For Couples* by Dennis Rainey and Barbara Rainey
- *Pillow Talk for Couples: Drawing Closer Before the Lights Go Out* by Les Parrott and Leslie Parrott
- *The 5 Sex Needs of Men & Women* by Gary Rosberg, Barbara Rosberg, and Ginger Kolbaba (notice the numbers and then, WOW, three auhors — is that a sex need?)
- *Love & Respect: The Love She Most Desires; The Respect He Desperately Needs* by Emerson Eggerichs
- *I Kissed Dating Goodbye: A New Attitude Toward Romance and Relationships* by Joshua Harris
- *Holding Hands, Holding Hearts: Recovering a Biblical View of Christian Dating* by Richard Phillips and Sharon Phillips
- *What Every Man Wants in a Woman; What Every Woman Wants in a Man* by John Hagee, Diana Hagee, Charles Burr, and Sandra Burr

Some authors take it one step further and actually make a separate "His" book and "Hers" book. These folks really know how to keep the cash flowing in...

Here are some I see in the Christian Living Section:

Shaunti Feldhahn and Jeff Feldhahn
- *For Women Only: What You Need to Know about the Inner Lives of Men*
- *For Men Only: A Straightforward Guide to the Inner Lives of Women*

Gary Smalley and Barbara Rosberg
- *Connecting with Your Husband*
- *Connecting with Your Wife*

James Dobson and Patrick Morley
- *What Wives Wish Their Husbands Knew About Women*
- *What Husbands Wish Their Wives Knew About Men*

There truly is no limit to how far you can go.

Remember, people are buying these books. Maybe you have.

- *What Wives Wish Their Husbands Knew about Sex: A Guide for Christian Men* by Ryan Howes, Richard Rupp, and Stephen Simpson (hopefully not homos)
- *What Husbands Wish Their Wives Knew About Money* by Larry Burkett
- *What Wives Wish Their Husbands Knew About Homeschooling* (Audio) by Scott Somerville

The next technique appeals to individuals whose worries are out of this world. The supernatural is exciting to write about — nothing can be proved, so you're never wrong and you're always an expert. The topics normally cover anything from creationism to eschatology, from demonology to angelology, from cursing to healing, from the prophetic to the pathetic.

For every vision that an author claims to have, you can find one in another book right beside it that completely contradicts the first.

Another technique is geared for the appeal of the intelligentia. The seminary students love these books. These books aren't normally in the Christian Living Section, but they deserve a mention nonetheless.

Toss in a fresh term for an old idea and the masses reply with enthusiasm. The new knowledge is hoarded over the ignorant until they catch on and then it is time for the next vocabulary switch.

You've seen the words, mostly ending in -isms, -ics, and -ologies — you didn't know what they meant at first, but after you heard them a couple times, you realized they were old news or simple concepts wrapped up in fancy packages.

Then you flaunted them at the next house group. Often times these books are entry-level versions of systematic theology.

Here is my list of "big words" that my fellow Christians have used to hoard knowledge over me or that authors have spent pages and pages explaining away — see how many you know:

Agnosticism	Eschatology
Amillenialism	Eternal Security
Annihilationism	Exegesis
Arminianism	Existentialism
Calvinism	Expiation
Complimentarianism	Fatalism
Consubstantiation	Fideism
Deism	Foreknowledge
Deontology	Free Will
Depravity	Gnosticism
Determinism	Hamaritology
Dichotomy	Hedonism
Dualism	Henotheism
Ecclesiology	Hermeneutics
Egalitarianism	Heterodoxy
Eisegesis	Homiletics
Election	Humanism
Empiricism	Immutability
Epistemology	Infralapsarianism

Justification	Premillennialism
Limited Atonement	Preterition
Materialism	Rationalism
Millennium	Regeneration
Modalism	Sacerdotalism
Monergism	Sanctification
Monophycitism	Skepticism
Monotheism	Sola Fide
Naturalism	Sola Gratia
Neo-orthodoxy	Sola Scriptura
Nestorianism	Soteriology
Objectivism	Sovereignty
Omnipotence	Subjectivism
Omnipresence	Supralapsarianism
Omniscience	Synergism
Ontology	Teleological
Panentheism	Tetrgrammaton
Pantheism	Theism
Pedobaptism	Theodicy
Palegianism	Theophay
Perseverance	Total Depravity
Pluralism	Transubstantiation
Pneumatology	Trichotomy
Polytheism	Tritheism
Postmillennialism	Typology
Pragmatism	Unitarianism
Predestination	Universalism

As the previous technique actually proved to require an amount of knowledge and understanding, many authors began to make their own simple words and build entire world views from them. These titles manifest themselves in genres like New Age theology, postmodernism, relativism, emergent philosophies, and so on.

Lastly, many authors find the act of name-tossing very lucrative.

What is a name worth?

Apparently a lot.

Consider the following:

- *The Prayer of Jabez: Breaking Through to the Blessed Life* by Bruce Wilkinson and David Kopp
- *The Elijah Task* by John Sandford and Paula Sandford
- *The Diet of Daniel: A 10 Day Diet to Blessed Health, Weight Loss, and Fitness* by Ernest Edsel
- *Having a Mary Heart in a Martha World* by Joanna Weaver

STUPID CHURCH BOOK HYPE: COVER

The cover, more so than the title, might very well exist as a part of the marketing scheme rather than simply one of the four main principles of hype — again, the principles are so closely entwined; however, for many customers, the reassuring glimpse from the smiling author on the front might be the single-most important component of their next impulse purchase.

But how does anyone trust these smiles? They're so obviously schmoozy. We don't trust car salesmen, so why do we trust these authors? For me, it's often that pretentiously welcoming smile on the cover that sets me running fast in the other direction.

But I guess they get a good amount of positive feedback with that smile.

But I'll bet there's even a college-level course in the basement of that famous book publisher:

Selling Crap by Wrapping it in Colorful Cloth 101

It deals with designing those flashy covers on the Bible-zines that grab my attention.

It deals with the minimalistically-hip, all-white covers that say, "Let's just keep it real."

It deals with recognizing when to place a pretty picture on the cover versus a scientific one, or when to plaster on said cover your enhanced, inviting smile versus a solemn gaze out into the lights.

I have found at least five classifications of covers: the cool contemporary-fresh look, the ancient book of knowledge look, the serene little book of life advice from the experts look, the scientific look, and the John Earl Shoaff or Tony Robbins cover — the original Face Book.

The following pages will help illustrate the different concepts.

Cool Contemporary-Fresh Titles

- *Revolution* by George Barna
- *The Voice of Acts: The Dust Off Their Feet: Lessons from the First Church* by Chris Seay
- *Divine Intervention: Encountering God Through the Ancient Practice of Lectio Divina* by Tony Jones
- *Through Painted Deserts: Light, God, and Beauty on the Open Road* by Donald Miller
- *Untamed: Becoming the Man You Want to Be* by Xan Hood
- *Jesus Freaks: Martyrs: Stories of Those Who Stood for Jesus: The Ultimate Jesus Freaks* by dc Talk
- *Blue Like Jazz: Nonreligious Thoughts on Christian Spirituality by Donald Miller*
- *Jesus Freaks: Revolutionaries: Stories of Revolutionaries Who Changed Their World: Fearing God, Not Man* by dc Talk
- *The Last Stupid Church Book You'll Ever Read* by Benjamin Samples and James Townsend
- *An Emergent Manifesto of Hope* by Doug Pagitt and Tony Jones
- *Gateways To God* by Pete Lowman
- *unChristian: What a New Generation Really Thinks about Christianity. . .and Why It Matters* by David Kinnaman and Gabe Lyons
- *Everything Must Change: Jesus, Global Crises, and a Revolution of Hope* by Brian McLaren
- *Summoned to Lead* by Dr. Leonard Sweet
- *Every Day Deserves a Chance: Wake Up to the Gift of 24 Hours* by Max Lucado
- *Plastic Jesus: Exposing the Hollowness of Comfortable Christianity* by Eric Sandras

Cool Contemporary-Fresh Covers

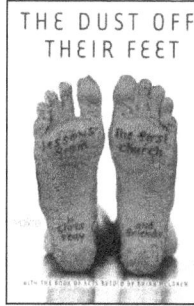

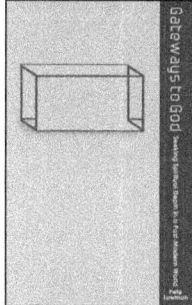

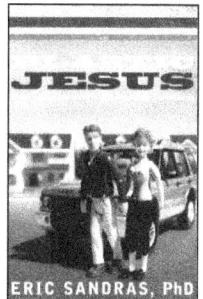

Ancient Book of Knowledge Titles

- *Saint John in Exile* by Dean Jones
- *The Secret Message of Jesus* (audiobook) by Brian D. McLaren
- *Early Christian Doctrines* by J.N.D. Kelly
- *Lost Christianities: The Battles for Scripture and the Faiths We Never Knew* by Bart D. Ehrman
- *The Lost Gospel of Judas Iscariot: A New Look at the Betrayer and Betrayed* by Bart D. Ehrman
- *The Lost Gospel: The book of Q and Christian Origins* by Burton L. Mack
- *The Didache: Text, Translation, Analysis, and Commentary* by Aaron Milavec
- *Ancient Christian Devotional: A Year of Weekly Readings* by Cindy Crosby and Thomas C. Oden
- *Jesus Among Other Gods* by Ravi Zacharias
- *The Revelation of Truth* by John Hagee

Ancient Book of Knowledge Covers

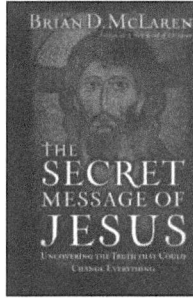

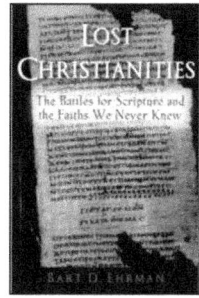

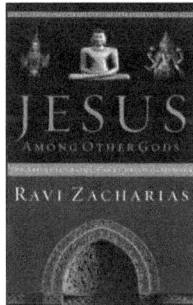

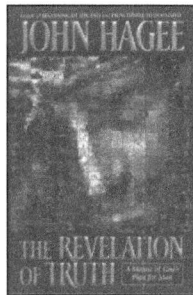

Serene Little Book of Life Advice Titles

- *The Knowledge of the Holy* by A.W. Tozer
- *My Daily Devotion: God's Promises for Joyful Living* by Stephen L. Carter
- *Experiencing His Presence: Devotions for God Catchers* by Tommy Tenney
- *Night Light* by Dr. James Dobson and Shirley Dobson
- *Rest Assured: Devotions for Souls in a Restless World* by Nancy McGuirk
- *God Calling* by A.J. Russell
- *A Life of Obedience* by Andrew Murray
- *Of Earth and Sky: Spiritual Lessons from Nature* by Thomas Becknell
- *Christianity: A New Look at Ancient Wisdom* by David J.H. Hart
- *Wild at Heart* by John Eldredge
- *Basic Christianity* by John Stott
- *A Look at Life from a Deer Stand: Hunting for the Meaning of Life* by Steve Chapman
- *I Know You Are Hurting* by Zig Ziglar
- *Grieving God's Way* by Margaret Brownley
- *Confessions of a Grieving Christian* by Zig Ziglar
- *Good Morning, Holy Spirit* by Benny Hinn

Serene Little Book of Life Advice Covers

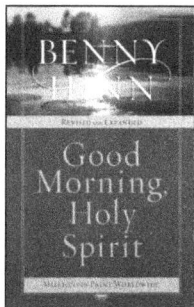

The Knowledge of the Holy
A. W. TOZER

My Daily Devotion
GOD'S PROMISES for JOYFUL LIVING

TOMMY TENNEY
Experiencing His Presence
DEVOTIONS FOR GOD CATCHERS

NIGHT LIGHT
DR. JAMES & SHIRLEY DOBSON

REST Assured

THE INSPIRING CLASSIC
GOD CALLING
EDITED BY A.J. RUSSELL

A LIFE OF
Obedience
Andrew Murray

Of Earth and Sky
SPIRITUAL LESSONS FROM NATURE

Christianity
A NEW LOOK AT ANCIENT WISDOM

JOHN ELDREDGE
WILD at HEART

BASIC Christianity
John R.W. STOTT

A Look at Life From a Deer Stand
Hunting for the Meaning of Life
Steve Chapman

I KNOW YOU ARE HURTING
ZIG ZIGLAR

Grieving God's Way
Margaret Brownley

CONFESSIONS OF A GRIEVING CHRISTIAN
ZIG ZIGLAR

BENNY HINN
Good Morning, Holy Spirit

97

Scientific Titles

- *The Case for a Creator: A Journalist Investigates Scientific Evidence That Points Toward God* by Lee Strobel
- *Unlocking the Mystery of Life: The Scientific Case for Intelligent Design* (DVD) by Randolf Productions Inc.
- *The Limitations of Scientific Truth: Why Science Can't Answer Life's Ultimate Questions* by Nigel Brush
- *The Ground and Grammar of Theology* by Thomas F. Torrance
- *Science and Theology: An Introduction* by John Polkinghorne
- *A Meaningful World: How the Arts and Sciences Reveal the Genius of Nature* by Benjamin Wiker and Jonathan Witt
- *By Design or by Chance?* by Denyse O'Leary
- *The Creation Hypothesis* by J.P. Moreland
- *Has Science Got Rid of God?* by John Blanchard
- *Executing the Basics of Healing* by Kenneth Hagin Jr.
- *Creation and Double Chaos: Science and Theology in Discussion* by Sjoerd L. Bonting
- *Back to Darwin: A Richer Account of Evolution* by John B. Cobb Jr.

Scientific Covers

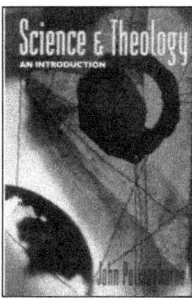

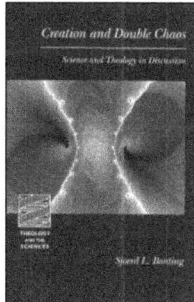

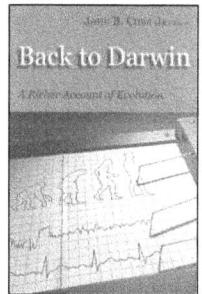

Face Book Titles

- *Become a Better You: 7 Keys to Improving Your Life Every Day* by Joel Osteen
- *Your Best Life Now: 7 Steps to Living at Your Full Potential* by Joel Osteeen
- *Get Out of That Pit: Straight Talk about God's Deliverance from a Former Pit-Dweller* by Beth Moore
- *Approval Addiction: Overcoming Your Need to Please Everyone* by Joyce Meyer
- *Conflict Free Living: How to Build Healthy Relationships for Life* by Joyce Meyer
- *8 Steps to Create the Life You Want: The Anatomy of a Successful Life* by Creflo A. Dollar
- *21 Days to Your Spiritual Makeover: Small Changes that Bring Results* by Taffi Dollar
- *How to Make Life Work: The Guide to Getting It Together and Keeping It Together* by Michelle McKinney Hammond
- *His Not Mine* by Bernard Palmer
- *You Are Not Your Own: Living Loud for God* by Jason Perry Steve Keels
- *Lessons from a Sheep Dog: A True Story of Transforming Love* by W. Phillip Keller
- *Don't Bet Against Me! Beating the Odds Against Breast Cancer and in Life* by Deanna Favre and Angela Elwell Hunt
- *You're All That! Understand God's Design for Your Life* by Paula White
- *Walking the Walk: Getting Fit with Faith* by Leslie Sansone
- *The DNA of Relationships: Discover How You Are Designed for Satisfying Relationships* by Gary Smalley, Greg Smalley, and Michael Smalley
- *Change Your Life: Achieve a Healthy Body, Heal Relationships, and Connect with God* by Becky Tirabassi

Face Book Covers

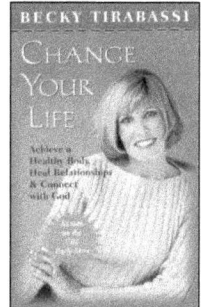

More Face Book Titles

- *Releasing Your Potential* by Myles Munroe
- *A Generous Orthodoxy* by Brian D. McLaren
- *From a Mess to a Miracle* by Kimberly Daniels
- *Reposition Yourself: Living Life Without Limits* by T.D. Jakes
- *Life Overflowing: 6 Pillars for Abundant Living* by T.D. Jakes
- *It Will All Come Out in the Fire* by T.D. Jakes
- *Silent No More: Bringing Moral Clarity to America While Freedom Still Rings* by Rod Parsley
- *Culturally Incorrect: How Clashing Worldviews Affect Your Future* by Rod Parsley
- *The Total Money Makeover: A Proven Plan for Financial Fitness* by Dave Ramsey
- *Living the Extraordinary Life* by Charles F. Stanley

More Face Book Covers

LAST STUPID CHURCH BOOK

Cool is in. Or maybe "phat" is in. Or maybe it is a brand new word.

The thought is the same though: a large part of any crowd has always thought that there needs to be a rebellion against the status quo and that it is time to move on to a new paradigm — to something new under the sun.

Today's institutions were yesterday's revolutions. And the trend shows no sign of changing.

People today seem to be diluting Christianity with a universal acceptance of anti- or pseudo- Christian beliefs and activities, an over-reliance on relating to the world, and a minimum dependence on the Bible and its authority.

People eat up anything relating to Gnostic thought or "secret" Christianities. If a book mentions the gospel of Thomas, it's an instant bestseller. Not particularly because Gnosticism or any apocryphal gospels have anything better or more substantial to offer. They just have that mark of "taboo" on them, exuding this aura of secrecy that is instantly appealing to itchy-eared folks.

It's kind of like whispering. If you really want people to pay attention to what you're saying, just start whispering it; and everyone near you will try to listen while appearing to not do so. When you hear a whisper, you think you're not supposed to hear what's being said, so you listen harder.

Likewise, when people market inconsistent, fake Christianities with flabby theology, and the Church objects, people gobble it up all the more. Not because it's good stuff, but just because there are objections.

But maybe there are good grounds for objecting.

104

STUPID CHURCH BOOK HYPE: MARKETING AND FOLLOW-UP

Once you have the story, a catchy title, and a killer cover, the next and probably most important step deals with marketing and follow-up.

The marketing plan is responsible for getting the book out to the masses. The follow-up plan makes sure the hype can continue for future purchases.

Each works to put cash-into-pocket at the highest rate of giddy-up — and each really works.

I have seen it a hundred times:

Brandon is a well-intentioned Christian.

He is hoping to further the plight of Christianity.

He begins reading a book that genuinely touches his heart.

His life is changing.

He becomes a better person.

He becomes a more successful person.

Perhaps he has simply developed a fresh and new outlook.

He has found one of those books you are unable to put down.

He finishes the book in less than a week.

He is still high on the developments it brought about in his life.

He has an idea — probably an inspiration.

"I need to get this idea out to my brothers and sisters."

At the next house group or Bible study, Brandon casts the idea of introducing the book for further study.

His Christian siblings, eager to please the LORD in new and fresh ways, respond:

"This could be neat" or "Yeah, I have heard of that book, too."

Then it begins. The Bible study, weakened because of its apparent lack of relevance, yields to the book study, ready to take on the current topics and events of today's church.

This Book Changed My Life

At the last "contemporary-fresh" church we attended, my wife and I went to the 20-30something's Bible Study class after Sunday Worship. We sat down with our Bibles, and the leader — probably someone just like Brandon — asks his wife,

"Can you hand them a copy?"

He turns to me.

"Hi!" he says, with that whitening-strip-enhanced, award-winning smile. "We have been going through Zig Ziglar's *God's Way is Still the Best Way*. It has truly changed my life — made me a better, more successful person!"

A smarter, more patient version of who I am today, I smiled, thanked his wife for the copy, and opened it to the first page with ink.

It read:

"You, _____, by following these concepts will be able to experience success God's way, which is the best way!"

Along with the group, I flipped over to Chapter 11: Sharing Christ With Others.

My wife and I and fifteen others sat in the room that day and listened to the leader explain how to share Christ with a special pin or an invite card — a business card advertising your church's "great message and beautiful music." (page 151)

I should have left my Bible at home.

However, this experience is being repeated all over the world, and in the United States in particular. We don't really want to focus on the Bible so much as just have it in the same room. If we can just reference a couple of verses here and there, and then get back to this really engaging, challenging book, then we seem to think we've done our job in incorporating the Scriptures into our lives .

But for a better indication of what really does challenge us, take a look at what we veer *away* from reading. It's always the Bible that seems to collect dust when it stands against the latest pop-Christ bestseller.

Does this scenario represent a deviation?

Again, when defending the faith against cults and other out-groups, it is so easy to claim that reliance upon sources *other* than Scripture is a basis for destruction.

So why shouldn't this same assertion be applied a little closer to home?

The answer, of course, is that if it *were* applied, we'd be losing a *lot* of money. It's just not profitable for authors to use the Bible, and the Bible only, as a church resource.

When a well-known writer, perhaps an author of previous bestsellers, spits out his or her newest book, pastors and other church leaders will begin their consumer-campaign. They encourage their fellow congregation members to buy the new book; Sunday morning announcements include words of testimony and praise concerning the new book, and how it has changed this person's life or that person's career. The pastor will heft it in his hand as if it were worth its weight in gold.

Discussion groups will begin to form, where it is suggested that each member of the group buy his or her own copy of the book.

After the initial purchases, the author of the book has no doubt published a guidebook and/or journal, with which to aid the readers in gaining new and fresh insights.

The existence of such reading groups in churches, along with countless references to the new book in sermons, bulletins, and external trendy Christian magazines guarantees the success of the author.

One need only think of Rick Warren, and walk the aisles of a bookstore where his books are kept, to see evidence of this.

I myself easily found the titles — shelved next to the near-life-sized poster of Rick Warren's head displaying that "cha-ching" smile. On the back of the dust jacket for *The Purpose-Driven Life*, Lee Strobel, Author of *The Case for Christ*, proclaims:

> *If you only read one book on what life is all about — make it this one! This book is life-changing. Rick Warren is absolutely brilliant at explaining our real purpose on earth and stating profound truths in simple ways. Give this book to everyone you care about. Believe me, you'll never be the same after reading this! What a gift!*

108

It would have been my hope that such well-known, respected authors were pointing to the Bible with such exalting language.

But, if Warren's book is *that* simple to understand, then maybe I will buy it — I mean this is life-changing stuff!

But wait, just flipping through the *Resources* section of *The Purpose-Driven Life* I see I may also need the following:

- *The Purpose-Driven Church*
- The Purpose-Driven Website, *www.purposedrivenlife.com*
- *The Purpose-Driven Life Journal*
- *The Purpose-Driven Life Scripture Keepers Plus*
- *The Purpose-Driven Life Album*
- *The Purpose-Driven Life Video Curriculum*
- *Foundations: 11 Core Truths to Build Your Life On*
- *Doing Life Together*
- *Planned for God's Pleasure*
- *Rick Warren's Ministry Toolbox*
- *Purpose Driven Seminars*
- *Your First Steps to Spiritual Growth*
- *The Purpose-Driven Life Health Assessment*
- *Celebrate Recovery*
- *Kingdom Builders*
- *40 Days of Purpose*

Before I handed Warren $17.99 for *The Purpose-Driven Life* alone, I decided to do a little on-line research to see how complex this undertaking might become.

The Purpose-Driven Life website did provide me with a 30 day, 90 day, or 1 year Bible reading plan. (By the way, I chose the 30 day plan — I figured if I could tackle *The Purpose Driven Life* in 40 days, I should be able to tackle the Word in 30.)

It also provided help with developing my life-purpose statements, but there is a little more information necessary for completion of each of the five purposes.

The following books are recommended for further study:

Worship
- *Experiencing God*
- *Worship Old and New*
- *Praying for Purpose for Women*
- *The Way of the Worshiper*
- *Love Him in the Morning*
- *Renovation of Heart*

Fellowship
- *Connection (on relationships)*
- *Conversations on Purpose for Women*
- *Boundaries*
- *Boundaries in Marriage*

Discipleship
- *How People Grow*
- *Pursuit of Holiness*
- *Pathways to Purpose*
- *A Resilient Life*
- *Rebuilding Your Broken World*
- *The Life God Blesses*
- *The Incredible Patience of God*
- *Personal Bible Study Methods*
- *The Power to Change Your Life*
- *The Life You've Always Wanted*
- *Understanding Who You Are*
- *Margin*

Ministry
- *Improving Your Serve* (I would love to see the Christian driving book entitled: *Improving your* Swerve! We can only hope, right?)
- *What You Do Best — In the Body of Christ*
- *Living the Life You Were Meant to Live (or Discipleship)*

Evangelism
- *The Master Plan of Evangelism*
- *The Case for Christ*
- *The Case for Faith*
- *Mere Christianity*
- *What on Earth Am I Here For?*

What started out as a $20.00 investment in a single book has ended up with more reading than the first year of law school and over $500 in book purchases! My 40 days of purpose now have me in debt with over 30 additional purchases. Thankfully there is a book for that as well.

We fall right in to the trap, jubilant with bliss, falling clear down to the pongee sticks with big smiles on our faces, thinking that we are investing not only in the strength of our Christian walk, but in the lives of some of world's most dedicated Christians.

Hook, Line, and Sinker
Greg Stielstra wrote the book on how the campaign works: *PyroMarketing: The Four-Step Strategy to Ignite Customer Evangelists and Keep Them for Life*.

What a sleazy title.

"Customer Evangelists." Now there's a phrase that'll just turn your insides to ash.

Isn't this the kind of stuff that made Jesus take whip-making classes? We're making God's kingdom a matter of profiteering, marketing, and consumerism, complete with 6 Sigma and S.W.O.T. analysis.

Stielstra could have just called his book, *Hook, Line, and Sinker: How to get them to bite, and then keep them on the hook.*

And if there is anyone who would be the expert on this, it would be him— he is the mastermind behind *The Purpose-Driven Life* campaign and the Senior Marketing Director at Zondervan Publishing, one of the largest publishers to fill the aisles of the Christian Living section. On his public Resources page (at pyromarketing.com), the PyroMarketing Overview describes his process in four simple steps.

To illustrate, let's review these steps as they are presented on his public website:

Gather the Driest Tender

These people have the lowest ignition temperature relative to your product. The slightest heat from your marketing causes them to light and burn hot. This is the only group whose ignition temperature is within reach of traditional advertising.

Touch it with the Match

Let people experience your product or service. If you want prospects to laugh, don't tell them you're funny; tell them a joke. Experience is hotter than advertising and can ignite even the mildly interested.

Fan the Flames

This means equipping your customers to spread your message more effectively through word-ofmouth. Personal influence is hotter than advertising or experience and the only way to convert the apathetic masses. Reach them by leveraging the power of passionate customer evangelists.

112

Save the Coals

> *Keep a record of the people you find with your marketing so that each new campaign builds equity you can tap in the future.*

I have fallen victim to the strategy time and time again. We all have. That's why advertising works: it has years of psychological research and experimentation backing it up, knowing how to affect mass audiences.

But really, was that last Stupid Church Book you read really *that* life-changing?

Or were you manipulated the same way I have been?

You bought the book everyone was raving about, read it, maybe even liked it well enough, but your life has gone on just the same.

And maybe your life isn't so bad to begin with.

Part of these guys' strategy is to convince you that your life needs bettering in the first place.

Then you can buy their book which tells you how to do it.

But again, if we're honest to the point of personal conviction, not much transformation will ever occur from reading any of these books (except the financial kind of transformation regarding the authors' bank accounts).

We're Not Alone, Here

Is there no voice for those enslaved by Stielstra's malintentions? Thanfully, there is Tim Challies, a reformed Christian author with an online blog, who accurately explains the three ways that Stielstra's approach takes advantage of the Christian community (please see more at www.challies.com):

Naivety

This approach dupes Christians into becoming marketers, not for a book, but for a marketing approach, and ultimately for a profit-driven corporation. This marketing approach is supposed to work as easily with any product as with what is a supposedly-biblical book. There is nothing inherently Christian about the approach and it has no biblical basis.

Ignorance

This approach also benefited from the ignorance of evangelical Christians, that they were not able to see beyond the marketing and see a book that was, in many places, clearly unbiblical and which said little that had not already been said before, either by Christian or secular writers. Were Christians properly-educated in the Scriptures, this approach would fall flat.

Pragmatism

This approach is, at its heart, pragmatic. This is the charge that has long been leveled at the Church Growth Movement, that success becomes the ultimate arbiter of truth rather than the Word of God. In a sense all marketing is pragmatic, especially when it is designed to sell a product.

First came the book, then came the guidebook, then came the journal, then came the calendar, then came the devotional book, then came the book geared towards teens, parents, churches, then came the suggested reading — of course the authors are watching out for their buddies and the rest of the Christian Consumer Machine.

I'm just waiting for that Purpose-Driven breakfast cereal.

What do you gain from these Church Books?

Honestly...

A great number of the Church Books are half-hocked duplications of secular motivational titles with a verse or two (or two hundred) added and discussed so that the general nature of the story is bent toward the culture of Christianity.

Christian authors are making a *killing* off of putting old wine into new wineskins.

I wonder what Jesus would have to say about that...

Words & Notes, Books & Music: Some Help for Those Who Couldn't Hack It

Although we've focused on the literary aspect of Christian marketing, our media-based entertainment needs don't stop with pages and covers. We experience similar wiles in the music industry, too. I love walking into the CD section of the bookstore — the new trend of getting all your media in one place, I guess — and glancing through the shelves. I can almost predict the band's music just by looking at the album cover.

I continue through the aisles and discover many different sections. There is the rock section (one of my favorites), the alternative section, rap, country, musicals, soundtracks, foreign, classical, the list goes on.

Then there is the Christian section.

Think just for a minute.

What does rock and roll sound like?

What does rap sound like?

What does country sound like?

And now, what does Christian sound like?

Is there a Christian sound to music?

In all of God's diverse creation, does it seem logical, even believable that we Christians who enjoy a cymbal on a high-hat with a suped-up tempo must content ourselves with the sounds of DC Talk and WOW Worship?

Where's my snare?

Similar to the segregation amongst Christian titles and the rest of the bookstore, why is music sectioned out into genres depending on sound, but then split up based on religion?

Furthermore, why do you find albums like early U2, P.O.D. or MxPx in the "secular" rock sections? My apologies to MxPx. There normally isn't a punk section at the CD shops where we live.

These albums have Christian-oriented lyrics.

P.O.D. and MxPx both "claim" Christianity.

Is Christian music different than secular music?

Here, do we claim separate-but-equal?

It's not that I want Sam Walton or Mr. Barnes and Mr. Noble or Mr. Turner calling me and giving me their opinions of why music and books are sectioned off like this.

It's just that I want people, especially authors, bands, labels, publishers, churches, and Christians in general to take a look at what is going on.

In times past, P.O.D. was a very popular band in both the secular and Christian markets. Their music was, and to some extent, still is enjoyed by thousands at festivals like Cornerstone or as they tour with other big-name bands outside of today's accepted Christian arena.

Why are they in the secular section?

A Stupid Church Book authored by the likes of some popular Christian musician might try to explain away the notion of Christian music with something like this:

> **...Christian music is not about writing songs with a good message. It's about letting the Spirit sing through you. We want to meet people where they're at, and love on them without reservation. We need to reach out to the world. And if our God is the God of creation, and if music is a representation of that creation, then our music should be completely freakin' awesome — even by the standards of the world!**

> **...Christian music is about reclaiming what's "cool" from the devil, and giving it back to God as praise and glory!**

Writing, likewise, *is* a way many authors reveal or present themselves, their thoughts and their ideas — and there are many great books out there that illustrate the point that there are a large number of talented authors with great ideas.

A book, though, is essentially art — both the book created by the

Christian and the one created by the pagan. Incidentally, Christian bestsellers have only to compete with other Christian titles. When the Christian aisle exists as its own miniature bookstore, sectioned off with all the similar tags of its big-brother bookstore, you realize that we Christians might simply be mimicking the world by putting a weak coat of Christian paint on rusty secular ideas.

And in reality, isn't this kind of a motive, if not *the* motive, for writing Christian material, and playing Christian music? Because, if we're going to be honest, most of the material passed off onto society today as "Christian" in nature, is really sub-par as far as skill itself goes.

And it's really, amazingly, extremely cheesy.

One conclusion that could be reached from this catastrophe is that, from the wide array of very talented artists in the world, those who find themselves to be somewhat missing the mark, so to speak, or those who, for whatever reason, are unable to hack it in the "real world," can simply strut themselves and their low-grade cheese right over to the "Christian" market and peddle their wares there.

Let's face it. The Christian market is an easier industry. People are basically making *billions* saying the same thing that's been said for centuries.

Nothing new.

The Bible has a whole book on it — check out Ecclesiastes. It's all about the fresh packaging.

Say you write a fantasy story. But when it's finished, you realize that, in comparison to the market, it's really a pretty crappy story.

So what do you do?

120

Here's an idea for you future charlatans out there: pick some Christian themes, weave them into the story, and sell it in the Christian section of the bookstore.

Problem solved. And you get a paycheck.

Sadly, this may be a part of what's going on in the Christian industry today. Granted, I'm not saying that *every* artist in the Christian industry is cheesy and not worth your time.

I'm just saying most of them are.

And even more frightening is the fact that we may be putting an ugly grey primer on an already beautiful metal-flake enamel.

How would your average Christian-based financial book stand up to a secular money-management book?

Dave Ramsey did put it all together pretty well, hitting both markets with his Financial Freedom series while even claiming that he has nothing new to say, just new packaging.

Let's continue with some more Stupid Church Book religiosity—a Christian artist may have this to say about his or her passion:

> **...the world may not understand our hope or our faith, and this may stand in the way of properly discussing many topics; however, as Christians, we should bring true skills to the music stands and stages, canvases and wheels, magazines and books. We should bring them in a way that illustrates the intelligence and power of Christians. Perhaps it is better said like this:**
>
> **We shouldn't rely on the world's understanding**

121

to provide the subject matter for Christianity; we should let Christianity shape our understanding of the world and provide the subject matter for lives...

Standing alone, that statement isn't too profound. It is easily agreeable and doesn't step on anyone's toes. However, if we would examine Christianity for a moment, and then consider the use of arts in our lives and worship, we would see that all too often we are short-cutting a more wonderful experience by comparing our goods to the emotionally-driven goofiness in the Christian Living section.

And shorting ourselves in the process.

Here is some more Stupid Church Book Cheesiness for you to munch on (as is normal for the genre, it may be well-written and psuedo-Christian even though it is leavened with worldly psychologies and humanistic philosophies). And while reading this, consider what's really being said beneath the mystical rhetoric:

...we come to our places of worship to join with others in a time of jubilee and happiness, and music is a key factor in setting a mood or conveying an emotion...

...a song, however, doesn't bring the presence of God. A fervent heart does. More often than not, these songs we listen to, and these books we read, are someone's life experiences. They are meaningful times in a person's life. They could also be times of happiness, sad-

a song doesn't bring the presence of God, a fervent heart does

ness, doubt, or survival. No matter the situation though, the piece of music or the book, art in general is often a direct extension of the writer's life. If the author of that powerful book, *11:23*, were a painter, he would have created a colorful expression of his situation on canvas. If he were a dancer, the motions of his body would have illustrated the emotions of his mind. If he were a sculptor, his hands would have shaped physical material around his intangible mood of the scary situation...

...indeed, some of the original notions of art are found when it is displayed in the future. A sad picture may bring tears again and again. A song may give you a feeling of hope each time you listen to it. A scary story might send chills up your back each time you read it...

All art is power.

...as Christians, therefore, we are stewards of the events that lead to a soul's salvation...

This is the appeal of Stupid Church book titles: it puts you in the driver's seat. It is also the reason we often buy them.

But don't stop just yet, the book will go on to say:

...you create the art out of the expression of your inner self. The viewer is confined by the piece as to what he is able to feel, but still he is able to allow it to "advise" his actions or "direct" his thinking. And

This is how we touch hearts

this is how we reach people with Christian music. This is how we touch hearts...

On this note, we fully recognize with what passion Stupid Church Book authors write.

...true art is the pure expression of an idea...

And the bodies of these books are. . .at least. . .full of ideas.

...in engineering, a bridge is built in order to span two plots of land. The bridge can be inventive, pretty, or even a masterpiece, but it still has to connect the two pieces of land. The whole project is confined in that it must accomplish this task. In a way, it can still be artistic,

Our work, our life's passion, our struggle and our fight, is to see souls saved

but unless the art fulfills the proper task, the work is useless. Our work, our life's passion, our struggle and our fight, is to see souls saved...

You still have to please the altruists. . .

...artists are often times confined to the fact that they must make money to survive, so they produce imitations or money-makers. Art is produced simply because we are creatures with ideas that we like to see materialized. If we stop half way through a piece, nothing is broken or ceases to work; we just haven't communicated our idea...

To this end, the Church Book authors feel that it is their *calling* to write. It is their way to reach the multitudes. It is a form of preaching that can be delivered and received well after the author has passed on. There may even be a very positive message.

> ...how much stronger is the personal demonstration of a peer's ideas through art than a tape with an age-old song and a group of people singing it for the thirtieth time?
>
> Does God despise hearing the old hymns and choruses?
>
> Doubtful.
>
> Where there is a mouth pronouncing His name, He is always glad.
>
> Would your congregation's heart be strengthened by a more personal expression of the people in it?
>
> I imagine so.
>
> Would God look upon it with a smile?
>
> I think yes.
>
> This expression is where art comes in. It is the purest form of releasing that which God has put within you.
>
> Dancers dance!
>
> Singers sing!
>
> Painters paint!

Sculptors sculpt!

Thespians act!

Musicians play!

Authors write!

And Shrubbers Shrub! Oh right!

...May God make joyful the world around you.

These actions aren't something we do in place of cleaning the carpet or designing bridges. Rather, they are something that we do to give God glory and proclaim His name among the land. They are something we do because it is the most intrinsic nature of who we are. Of who we were made to be...

What is in us comes out.

...to see that it blesses God should urge us to do it with great zeal, and we should attempt to continue on with magnificent skill so that it can increase. We should practice creating the physical concepts of the spiritual yearnings that are within us. These other things need to be done and many people are gifted in diverse areas, but we can't hide behind the fact that we were made for action...

to see that it blesses God should urge us to do it with great zeal

...in whatever area we place ourselves, our nature to act on the Word will come through...

...it is only fitting that we should concentrate on being the best at all we do in order to give us the tools to accomplish the task of making the visions or our minds reality...

Driven by the Creator of the world, why are Stupid Church Book authors producing works that seldom achieve success outside of the Christian Living section? (Kudos, though, to you Stupid Church Book authors who have seen world-wide success with your pseudo-Christian titles.)

No less than two things are going on here:

1. Most writers cater to and thrive off of the niche market of Christianity, and

2. Some of the best authors out there in the rest of the bookstore are Christians (and possibly ashamed to admit it) who simply do what they do better than others because they are Christians.

Before I get slammed for not noting that we should be a people set apart from the world, why do we suppose that "set apart" means "something less"? Or why do we say it is something great, but not by the standards of the world?

When will the quality of a Christian production be the envy of the world because it is superb by Christian standards and greater than secular standards?

When it is the highest quality a production can become.

Is this a Christian goal or a secular goal?

Well, even if there *is* a separation between secular and sacred, we should consider that it's possible, and encouraged, for Christians to strive to be on the other side of the cheesiness coin. But it just seems like we've settled, in terms of quality.

Perhaps there may come a time when certain books are held in higher esteem because they are authored by a Christian. And by producing the best that we can produce, and by making the Christian perspective so much a part of our foundation as human beings, we can, by default, raise the bar of production, and leave the secular field wanting. The jury's still out, though.

Ironic, Don't Ya Think?

Do you find it ironic that you hold in your hands a Stupid Church Book that doesn't seek to change your life and make you a better person? Honestly, I didn't quite know how to pitch it. The minute I begin writing, I become the enemy — another Stupid Church Book author or "literary evangelist" (maybe you'd like to post that one with Wikipedia!) intent on defining Christianity in *my* terms — but how else do I do it?

I consider what I've said in this book as my attempt to boast in the Lord, fully recognizing the absurdity of my actions while fully acknowledging the life-changing power of His. If we believe there is a God, that the Holy Spirit is one Person of the Trinity, and that the Bible is God's, then we must believe it when this Bible illustrates that the Holy Spirit is our Teacher.

I also believe in the total sovereignty of God. I believe that God not only knows the happenings of all mankind, but that He *ordains* the happenings.

It's all in His hands.

While not discounting personal responsibility in the least, I believe that we who belong to God, belong not because of who we are or what we do, but because of who He is and because He has chosen and called us.

Really, I don't even see where we have the nature even to approach God until Jesus intervenes. And then, under the guide and call of a Perfect Shepherd, I can see no way to refuse such direction.

People love to rely on human responsibility when it comes to things we receive that we don't deserve. We would appreciate some form of personal responsibility. If you nearly avoid a car wreck because some jerk cuts you off, you would like to think it was your superior driving skill rather than just dumb luck.

This tendency comes back, at some point, to pride.

Nevertheless, when looking at salvation, I have not been convinced that any of us had much of anything to do with obtaining such a salvation.

From our end of things, it can be viewed more as dumb luck than anything (even though it was far, far more).

Sure, your hands were on the wheel and your foot on the gas, but it wasn't you turning or accelerating that allowed you to barely miss that car. Fortunately, Almighty God deserves the credit and so the only One we can boast in is the Lord.

I write all of this to reinforce the fact that I'm not trying to convince you of my way of understanding or convert you if you feel otherwise. If you are a Christian, it is because God chose you, not because you chose God, and not because anyone logically convinced you or philosophically malingered your presuppositions.

And it is not my intention to rely solely on logic when I challenge the presuppositions of the modern church-marketing movement.

But it is my intention to lay the message out that part of our problem today lies in not recognizing God's sovereignty. We can't make our lives better until we give them to God — or until He allows us to realize that they weren't ours to give in the first place.

And I think we can all agree that God is sovereign over His creation.

An understanding of this sovereignty brings things into perspective. When you realize that God directed you into that tough situation at work, or that unnecessary argument with your wife, it's a little tougher to curse the event, and a lot easier to simply lay it at the feet of the Lord.

After all, those things, too, end up working toward good for those folks who love God and are called according to His purpose.

But at some point in your logical understanding of Christianity and where you fit in with it all, you are going to run into the un-sovereign god that so many of the Stupid Church Book authors present (hopefully unknowingly or unwillingly).

This void created by serving this un-sovereign god slyly leads to an over-reliance on self and ultimately to the huge disappointment of Christianity — or, rather works-based Christianity.

When we lack trust in God's providence we begin to trust in our own council, and in our own plans. And we never have it figured out well enough to do that.

If you knew Morgan, you would find that she would be one of your best friends — a super nice girl, smart, outgoing, just great to be around. But she is very caught up in the culture of Christianity. She grew up in a typical curch, with a typical family, and led a very typical "churchy" life — devoted to a nominal, public Christianity, emphasizing works, chastity, and the church-camp, social-club mentality.

We have spent time talking together about God's omnipotent, omniscient, omnipresent nature along with the doctrines of sovereignty and grace, but we always end up on opposite sides of the chasm when I conclude:

"it has nothing to do with our efforts or works."

Speaking of the salvation of God's elect, she always deductively concludes that a world with God in total control would make us church-going automatons or robot rapists and android murderers.

Frankly, it's an old argument — and one I have heard a thousand times before:

> *If you believe in total sovereignty, then why do anything — why preach or teach?*

> *If you are bound by God's will, then you have no say in anything and you are basically a robot.*

> *If God has chosen you and if He will preserve you, then why not rape, pillage, plunder, and kill?*

Especially, why write a book, right? And furthermore, why would God allow Stupid Church Books to be published?

A little ironic, don't ya think?

I suppose it's just how God set it up.

132

"Jesus Extract" and the Word, Made from Concentrate

It is true, at the heart of *some* Church Book purchases is a quest for greater knowledge and understanding. But, at the heart of *many* Church Book purchases is a concern for personal well-being. Especially purchases in the self-help section.

Given that God is sovereign, we hold on to a lot more worry than is necessary. We also rely on many different ideas, techniques, and knowledge to overcome the multitude of troubles plaguing the Christian community. What if there was a way to strike right at the heart of these issues?

Has a Church Book ever been written that sufficiently tackles the realistic concerns of our collective Christian community?

These questions bring to mind a discussion I had with my sister-in-law, Sharon. I understand things a little differently than she does. She always encourages me to "extract the Jesus" from things.

"Jesus Extract"

One Sunday, after listening to a sermon that blatantly lacked any hint of Biblical backing, I began discussing the several related Church Book topics with my family in an attempt to differentiate between authors' opinions and Biblical truths. Sharon mentioned how the process of discernment involved assimilating what a preacher, teacher, or author had to say into three buckets:

1. useful and Biblical
2. useful but non-Biblical
3. not useful (either Biblical or non-Biblical)

The last bucket can be tossed.

The second bucket can be utilized as long as it doesn't conflict with Christian values.

The first bucket is the good stuff to keep — the "Jesus Extract."

Lemon extract is just a bit of lemon in an alcohol-based concoction. Just like lemon extract, Jesus Extract is merely a hint of the real thing or a percentage of the true essence. Incidentally, a lot of Church Books are filled with a lot of Jesus Extract. Discernment might be better defined as differentiating between which authors output Jesus' Word and which authors output Jesus Extract.

But why spend time extracting (and hopefully, correctly) bits and pieces from Stupid Church Books when the Bible itself is collecting dust?

Capitalizing on the Bible, a majority of Christian Living authors simply use print as a way to further their "preaching."

On the shelf at the grocery store, just next to the Jesus Extract is another fine product of consumerized Christianity.

Word, made from Concentrate

Peter, a good friend of mine, equates so much of the input we receive from preachers, TV-evangelists, and authors as "the Word, made from concentrate." This product contains some little tidbit of Biblical truth — perhaps a verse or part of a verse — that is dried out of the Word for easy transportation. When it arrives on site, it is added with a lot of water in the form of emotionally saturated sermons or golf-cart inspired tales to produce a cheap drink — half juice/half Kool-Aid™ — to satisfy the masses. But something's missing.

As the Holy Spirit directs our lives, we are developed to conform to the reality that God makes for us. As we spend time in the world, the Holy Spirit reveals new knowledge and understanding to us. This might also occur as we read the Church Books or listen to the various teachings; it might also occur as we read *Engineering Times* or *The Wall Street Journal*.

When we live as true followers of Jesus, realizing His Word permeates into every area of our lives, then **all** things will develop our knowledge and understanding, whether it be through things in agreement with our faith or through things in opposition to it. It is not necessary to hold on to Jesus Extract or the Word, made from concentrate, and piece it together later with particular, specific information from other Stupid Church Books or maybe even the True Word.

Our lives and our walk with God will be our filter.

We will be able to appropriately judge all incoming information with the Word so that only what is useful is ingested.

It is not necessary to apply steps and rules extracted from Stupid Church Books to experience Christ-centered living.

When you truly follow Jesus, life no longer becomes a trial of what is and is not acceptable or what is and is not useful, but now everything is acceptable and useful, freeing you to build on all that dwells within and around you.

It's no longer about do's and don't's.

It's about conforming your life to something worth conforming to:

The Bible.

136

Not Another Stupid Church Book

Local bookstores and coffee houses are great places to meet people of different beliefs and mindsets. It never fails that I run into someone I used to attend Church with who, after steering away from the Faith for a while, were just supernaturally redeemed at the new mega church down the road (the one with pastels and cool contemporary-fresh worship songs).

Their eyes are glazed over.

"We meet twice a week for Discovery Group over at our place," they say. They have this almost pained look on their faces, as if they are hanging upon your approval of their new spiritual home. "Oh, and on Saturdays the Core Teams go out to the mall for CIA time."

Yeah, C.I.A.: Christ In Action.

They use those words that make you curious if they had actually joined some (official) cult. When I first saw the Benny Hinns, Joel Olsteens, and Rod Parsleys of the world starting their mega churches, I always wondered how magnificent their teaching and instruction must be — how it must just magnify and exalt the Lord.

However, upon attending one of the mega churches for a while, I was quickly reminded that it is not Christianity that sells; it is hype.

Let's face it, isn't one of the most striking aspects of Christianity the fact that it does *not* sell?

If we lived in the kind of world where the gospel did sell, there would be no need for the gospel. But in reality, we live in a world where God's truth is revealed to the "foolish" and the "least of these."

Anything that is widely sold can be seen, in effect, as being "world approved." What's that say about we who are to "hate the world," as John's epistle tells us? It seems that too many Church Book authors are seeking after the wrong approval.

And in the end, it is only the *hype* that sells. At this point, we have come to a crossroads.

Have we discerned that this lifestyle of Christian marketing is not spiritually profitable and it is time to turn the channel, or do we wait for the Jesus Extract?

Each situation is unique. Maybe the Good News will still surface.

Don't go hatin' on Joel, though. Lots of people are in it for the wrong reasons. Maybe he and the other Christian celebs are in it for the right ones. But like Paul said, the gospel gets preached either way.

So what's my beef with Church Books?

I mean, I know next to nothing about any of these authors.

But I tell you this: I don't trust people who look like used-car salesmen, metrosexuals, or women's daytime talk-show hosts.

138

But here's the well-done meat of it: on what grounds do the majority of purchasers blindly gather the molding fruit of these authors?

- By watching TV?
- By reading the dust jacket?
- By talking with friends?
- By the recommendation of their pastor?
- At the urging of the marketing strategy?

How often are these books read and examined with Scripture, apart from the aforementioned half-quotes, distortions, and misquotes? How often does Scripture even come into the picture, unless it's pasted on the cover to make a book more marketable?

So, what if you tagged this Christian Consumer Machine as the market-driven monster it is and steered clear of it? What if you stopped buying the books that your local mega-store, or mega-church, rather, was raving about? What if you saved some ink and left those better-life workbooks on the shelf?

I suppose there are at least three outcomes.

1. Things might stay the same:

   Your life may continue, just as it has, with you fighting the Christian fight: living day-by-day, interacting with people and addressing secular issues with Christian-based values, while strongly taking the Gospel to the world.

2. Things might get worse:

   As hunger sets in, you may begin to slide into secularity, as the world provides its own succulent cuisine.

But maybe, just maybe, something else will happen.

3. Things might get better:

Maybe you will find something greater in what you already have.

Maybe all the things that Church Books promised would begin to happen. In fact, maybe those stupid church books were doing the opposite of what they promised they would do. Maybe they were suffocating a faith that was begging you to let it breathe.

Maybe there's something to be said in embracing the simplicity of Christ's yoke.

If God takes from you this unfulfilling habit of seeking spiritual guidance from the peddled rags of pyro-marketers, then maybe something wonderful really will happen.

Maybe you'll see the Bible as your Church Book.

Shortcutting Christianity

The mass of Stupid Church Books out there today have served to shortcut the reality of Christianity. I do not doubt that there is some Biblical knowledge to be gained from them, and perhaps if all the Bibles were burned, then these books might hold some type of message.

But thankfully, the Bible is still with us.

And why not go to the source?

If this is the last Stupid Church Book we ever read, then perhaps we would really become the Church, we would really be in continual prayer and worship. And all those other great things that we Stupid Church Book authors promise would happen after reading our books — well, maybe they would really happen.

This is not to say that this book has any more power than theirs to solicit change or initiate it, but as Christians, we should strive to develop ourselves in this life that God has provided us in Christ.

Read the Bible!

Get lost in it.

Learn from it.

Too many of the Stupid Church Books ultimately distract us from the Bible. We should question whether time spent going through Rick Warren's study guides is better utilized than time spent in the Word.

Additionally, by the same token, I want to ask you another question.

Who are you becoming?

The individuals who spent time with Charles Taze Russell's *Scripture Studies* were called Russellites. They later became the Jehovah's Witnesses.

Those who followed the teaching of Joseph Smith became Mormons.

Should we go ahead and call a turd a turd, tagging the Warren-ites, Bell-ites, or McLaren-ites of today?

Even in the New Testament, people began to question whether believers were of Paul or Apollos. Why do we act as if our times and our generation are any different from the last?

These books cause divisions as they build up pastors and their theologies to near-deity levels. People begin talking about how "this book" changed their lives, or how they were never the same after reading "that book."

And it is never the Bible that they are talking about.

Furthermore, as many of these pastors apply pieces of Scripture far from their obvious contexts, the definition of Christianity is becoming so wide and variable that everyone should be a Christian. Incidentally, broadening the truth doesn't save more souls. Telling folks that there is no fire does not pull them out of a burning building.

Perhaps one of the largest snares of the devil is this culture that people call Christianity.

It is each new cultural shift, in what ever form it may take, that Stupid Church Book authors capitalize on.

It is tagging our culture as "Christianity" that makes us so weak.

Can't Stand to Reason
with the Scriptures

Let's get stupid!

Our poor reasoning (the reasoning, by the way, that we often use without realizing it) is often the result of what my more intelligent statistician friend equates to type I and type II error:

When you go to the doctors, they tell you that you have three days to live because of some time-released super-bacteria in your system.

You spend the next three days living life to the fullest. Maybe you go see all your relatives, or just spend some super quality time with those you care about. Or maybe you go do that one thing you couldn't get the guts to do while you were living, whether it was jump from a plane with a parachute or run naked down the beach.

Well, day four comes around, and, sure enough, you are alive!

You go back to the doctors and they recheck you from head

to toe. Oh my! Silly doctors! They hadn't diagnosed you correctly! It wasn't some deadly bacteria, it was just the chili you had eaten for dinner the other night! With proper diet and exercise, you are on your way to a long, healthy, happy life!

You have just experienced type I error. You perceived that something bad had happened, reacted to it (thankfully just by running naked down the beach!), and then realized that nothing bad had happened.

But next week, you notice a spot on your foot – some kind of puncture.

You run down to the hospital to see the doctors who, by the way, are feeling pretty bad for having just recently sent you through such a stressful few days. They check the wound, decide that it is just needs wrapped up, and off you go.

A few days later, as you're driving through McDonald's, you begin to get light-headed and dizzy.

Everything slowly fades to black.

After you have paid for it, but before you get your Happy Meal, you die.

The autopsy reveals that while you were running down the beach you had stepped on a syringe. It was full of some strange time-released super-toxin that kills you several days after you are injected with it.

You just experienced type II error. You perceived that nothing bad had happened, did not react to it, and then realized that something bad had happened and you missed it.

144

In both situations there has been an error.

Something that was wrongly perceived in your initial prognosis of a situation caused an improper understanding of the outcome. This improper understanding of the outcome might be the result of the following:

1. a weak or false premise
2. a deductive fallacy in arguing

You logically and rationally ran from one step to the next (as you should), though without realizing that there was a factual error — perhaps one dealing not with your perception or reaction, but possibly with that reality that exists outside of and beyond how we simply *see* things.

That's the problem we all run into when it comes to "reason." A person's logic can be flawless, and their convictions can be based on a perfectly integrated system of thought and belief.

But if there is just one overlooked, tiny inconsistency at the beginning of things, it will throw the whole train off the track miles down the road.

That's why people in cults, or people who adhere to any dogmatic, unbending, fanatic viewpoint are often so good at defending their position. For even though they have a small inconsistency somewhere in their thinking which causes the whole system to be in error, they have at least integrated that system and are prepared to defend it.

Sadly, most folks today have made logic and reason the measure by which they believe. But in doing so, they believe in something far more unbelievable than any system they may reject: the infallibility of their own minds.

Stevie Wonder is God

To see how some people can experience these errors in thought, take a look at these examples, and notice how a person's evaluation of objective data can lead to false assumptions:

Major premise
He who claims to be tall is tall.
Minor premise
Jake claims to be tall.
Conclusion
Jake is tall.

Some see this line of reasoning absurd, especially Jake's friend who knows that Jake is 4' 3" tall.

But let's replace *tall* with *Christian.*

Major premise
He who claims to be a Christian is a Christian.
Minor premise
Jake claims to be a Christian.
Conclusion
Jake is a Christian.

Similar reasoning, but few Christians would see the absurdity in this statement.

Blinded by the marketing, I'm sure.

But that's a problem we run into in a world that is, often by default, nominally Christian. And in this culture, it is near impossible to separate the wheat from the weeds.

Best leave it up to God.

Here is another approach to it. Put very simply, it may look like this:

Major premise
> All domesticated dogs are mean.

Minor premise
> Rolf is a domesticated dog.

Conclusion
> Rolf is mean.

The most evident problem here is that the first statement, "All domesticated dogs are mean," is far from the truth.

A bigger problem is that the conclusion may still be correct.

Rolf might be the meanest dog on the block. Actually, last week, he took a chunk out of my hind quarters while I was running through the neighborhood. But this fact in no way proves that "All domesticated dogs are mean." However, this fact does support the poor reasoning that happened to yield a correct conclusion in my particular scenario.

Consider this one, perhaps a little tougher:

Major premise
> If the streets are wet, then it has rained recently.

Minor premise
> The streets are wet.

Conclusion
> It has rained recently.

Sounds logical at first.

Because it is.

Logically, this conclusion is totally correct.

But wait!

What about a water leak or a flood? Or even the fact that you took your water hose out and personally sprayed the street down.

But more than likely, it really had rained.

Perhaps the biggest problem here is that we often find simple, rational, and realistic solutions with poorly-reasoned logic on a daily basis.

And the previously mentioned belief in the infallibility of our own minds is probably the main contributing force behind this problem.

When we rely on our reason to integrate and evaluate the premises, we automatically assume that we have collected *all* the information, and are in fact capable of performing true and accurate evaluations.

We are, however, *not* capable of coming to a correct spiritual assessment of our human situation without the help of God's Spirit.

We learn this premise-application technique early on in our lives, however, and, over time, we begin to apply the poor logic to tougher situations and end up with unrealistic solutions. Nevertheless, we accept the solutions because the logic we normally use normally works — our faith is in logic over, well, Faith. Let's continue:

Major premise
A capitol of a state is in that state.
Minor premise
Jacksonville is in Florida.
Conclusion
Jacksonville is the capitol of Florida.

Here, the premises are factually correct, but there is a flaw in the reasoning in reaching the conclusion.

You see, Tallahassee is the capitol of Florida (though Jacksonville is the most populated city).

One last logical syllogism — see if you can spot the flaw:

Major premise
> Love is blind.

Minor premise A
> God is Love.

Minor premise B
> Stevie Wonder is blind.

Conclusion
> Stevie Wonder is God.

As you're reading this, and your eyelids are getting heavy, and you're about to fall asleep, you may ask yourself:

Why are we looking at all of this statistical-philosophical-logical-crap?

Because, though it is wrought by our own flaws and blemishes, this same logic is why too many Stupid Church Book readers blindly fall for Stupid Church Book solutions every time!

It appears that a symptom, or side-effect, of the belief in our infallibility is the desire for things to be *presented* to us in ways that will only propogate the formula of premise-evaluation.

This is why we, by instinct, reach out for those "Seven Steps To Freedom" on the "New Release" shelf.

We want Stupid Church Book authors to present to us the proper premises, the proper formulas, and, ultimately, the proper evaluations, so that, in the end, it's not even *our* infallibility we're trusting in, but *theirs*.

In either case, however, we're decidedly *not* trusting in *God's* infallibility.

What happened to Faith?

Most of the time, these errors, among spiritual things anyways, stem from some form of eisegetical activities brought on by the Stupid Church Books. I am talking about reading things *into* the Word instead of out of the Word.

These books distract by leading people out into human-driven life.

And even if you're fueled by purpose, a human-driven life will wreck you every time.

Does God laugh at *Family Guy*?

I remember standing around at a house-warming party with some friends — Austin, a graphic-designer (the host), a couple of lawyers and their wives, and several others, mostly proclaimed Christians.

Before I even notice it, Austin has begun a discussion with me on the nature of God and whether or not He can feel all the feelings we can. More specifically, is God able to laugh at *Family Guy* or the *Simpsons* when they make a joke about Him?

Austin continues by reminding me how we realize our shortcomings and often laugh at them, but then asks can God, however, who has no shortcomings, find it humorous when we *perceive* a shortcoming and try to make a joke out of it?

When people view the Bible as the Answer Book, they find all sorts of questions without answers.

- Can God make a rock heavier than He can lift?
- Why won't God heal amputees?

150

- If God loves people, then why wouldn't everyone go to heaven?
- If you laugh at a retard, will your kids come out deformed and disabled?

When these questions cannot be answered sufficiently, it casts doubt on the power of the Word. Questions about the world and our place in it have been pondered from time immemorial. More problematic is the fact that, like the logical fallacies we discussed earlier, sometimes agreeable answers develop out of this kind of reasoning!

Unfortunately, it has become our status quo.

The Bible is not our User Manual. Unless you're into genocide, stoning unbelievers, and polygamy. (Okay, maybe it would be worth a look to see if we wanted to make the Bible our User Manual!)

But the Bible *is* a mystery that breathes inspiration, builds you up, convicts you, guides you, and shows you the things of God by revelation.

And conversation stemming from Bible perusal should never be discouraged. A good friend reminds me, "It is okay to discuss things like that if you are right!"

The only problem is that many times we are not — these times slowly reduce the gospel and its power.

Our approach to the Bible, reading into it what we want to see there, is kind of like dousing a plant with too much water. Our intentions are good, but now the once-fertile soil is watered down so much that nothing can grow from it.

When books claim to have the keys to success and the steps to understanding, are we to conclude that the Bible wasn't complete? Or perhaps we could conclude that we don't really want to spend time in the Bible; we just want to take others' words for it.

Nothing else will make you struggle with yourself, with God, and with life as much as you will when you read the Bible. All other books will either tell you that everything is okay, or that nothing is okay. That you are worthless, or that you are worthy.

In other words, every other book, being human in origin, lacks the depth that only God's revelation can provide. Only the Bible will tell you things that will rend your soul in order to heal it.

Only the Bible will tell you that everything *will* be okay, even if nothing is okay. That even though you *are* dirt, yet you could be so much more.

Incidentally, in addition to being the Answer Book, the Bible is also the Question Book. We come up with relevant questions to today's world, and consult the Bible, wanting it to give us cut-and-dry, black-and-white answers.

It is the Stupid Church Books that direct us into the many fantasy scenarios that cloud reality.

- How does teacher-led prayer in schools fit in with Christianity?
- What does the Bible have to say about online-churches?
- Should a Christian join a murdering Army?
- Can a homo be a preacher?
- Can said homo be a member of the congregation?
- Are birth-control pills Christian?

Again, these Church Books provide what the Bible never will, but what we very much would like it to.

These scenarios make the gospel into just that something extra that we have to tack on to our everyday modus operandi.

They make us ask, "how does Christianity fit in with our way of doing things?"

The problem with that question, however, is that a faith rooted in Jesus Christ should be your way of doing things. It doesn't "fit in," like a piece of a puzzle. Rather, the gospel breaks through, violently shattering your fragile preconceptions like glass, and forces you to pick up the pieces and conform your life to Jesus'.

But we buy books that support this "fitting-in" premise and then wonder why we don't get the results we want.

If the Bible were our Church Book, then perhaps we would begin to ask the right questions. Or perhaps we'd move beyond questions, into a life built purely on trusting in God and His goodness.

Back at the house-warming party, I quickly diffused my discussion with Austin by refusing to continue until we were discussing directly from the Bible. I insisted that we let the *Bible* direct our reasoning instead of relying on our *spiritual upbringing* in the culture of Christianity. We went upstairs and opened an online Bible and looked at Romans. We began by reading chapters 8 and 9, and also Isaiah 55, where we realize that we are a depraved people and that our ways are not God's ways.

The truth that our ways are not God's ways should be the first indication that we should not be trusting our own evaluations of things.

We did come to some new understanding, but I am sure it was somewhat tainted.

We still do not *really* know if God laughs at *Family Guy*.

We aren't sure if teacher-led prayer in school fits in with Christianity; neither did we read anything about online-churches or homo preachers. I encouraged Austin to regularly read Scripture and allow it to direct his questioning.

This is more along the lines of an exegetical activity — that is, moving *outward* with Scripture as the base.

But, having the Stupid Church Books, why would we ever need to do that?

Not Another Stupid Church Book, EVER

So, what would Christianity look like with the Bible as its Church Book?

The lists and steps of the self-help section may become yesterday's news. Formulas would be tossed out the window.

The lesson books on how to lay, sway, pray, and gray might go the way of the dinosaur.

The yearly hype of Christianity's next big thing might fizzle out to make room for reality.

Trends would dissipate. Consistency and simplicity would be rewarded.

It seems that the majority of the people I talk to claim to be Christian. It also seems that the majority of these people I talk to know nothing of what it means to follow Jesus. I hope this anomaly exists because people are unable to express their understanding and not because they have not experienced salvation.

My worry though, is that the latter is true.

The Word indicates that many who will call on the Lord are not His.

We hear stories of old of how Christians were persecuted and how prayer or other orders of worship were punishable by death.

If this were the case today, would so many individuals claim Christianity as their denomination on their dog tags?

I highly doubt they would.

The imperialization of Christianity, thus ushering in the dominance of what has been called "Christendom," is what caused all of this. The officializing of Christianity, although perhaps ordained in God's providence, has, as a side-effect, the nominal profession of millions, and the private devotion of the few.

There are many who profess Christ who do not trust Him. Many who love Him, but do not obey Him. And, worst of all, many that obey Him, but do not love Him.

+ + +

Christianity is so cool today. And there's something kind of weird about that.

For the younger half of Christianity, it can be slightly rebellious with punk clothes, a Jesus tattoo, and bitchin' music.

For the more dignified sorts, the regiment of attending service, the joy of financially supporting something, and the fellowship with other business owners, doctors, and lawyers are also very appealing.

For the rest of us lower class folks, there is a certain attraction to the routine of Church and the hope it provides throughout the week.

This culture called Christianity, like any good, well-oiled market-oriented business, has spread wide enough to fit and meet everyone exactly where they are.

It has also spread quite thin.

We've replaced the Bible with Bible-substitute, with congregants smearing their faiths with "I Can't Believe It's Not Bible!"

There is a vast chasm between the culture of Christianity and Christianity.

The morals, customs, and hopes of traditional Christianity may be attractive to many people. With the advent of so many varied types and kinds of society-driven Churches, there should be no reason that a person cannot find a style of supposed Christian living that is acceptable, even profitable, to their psyche and day-to-day disposition.

But, if promoting exclusivism, the phrase "style of Christianity" should be an oxymoron.

Christianity does have "flavors," as it spans cultures. Church services in Africa may look quite different than church services in Latin America, which in turn may look a lot different than ones in New England.

But these cultural flavors should not affect Christianity, in terms of the church as being a people "set apart."

A culture adapting to the Church is not the same as the Church adapting to a culture.

For instance, even though a certain culture may provide a different "taste" to its worship, if that culture promoted cannibalism, then that specific aspect of culture would have to go. Cannibalism would die out in the shadow of the Church, even though other aspects of the culture would remain to give the Church in that region its own unique flavor.

If, however, the Church accepted the cannibalism of that culture, then the Church would cease being the Church, and become something entirely different and distorted.

So when we approach the culture of Christianity today, we must, with the Bible, prayer, and faith as our guides, distinguish between the culture of the Church on the one hand, and the "church" of a culture on the other.

+ + +

The disconnect is between Christian Living and Christian Life.

Christian Living

At the heart of Christian Living are the steps and ways to become a better you.

Christian Living is the use of Christian values and culture to ease the tough social interactions that anyone may face day-to-day.

Christian Life

At the heart of Christian Life is Christ.

Christian Life is what is left when every other aspect of life has been curtailed to realize Christ as the perfect Savior He is.

At first read, the previous statements might sound like over-spiritual, organized religiosity that lacks real-world application. If so, what must change is your real-world view, not the simplicity of the Gospel.

158

Perhaps *you* must begin to move from Christian Living into Christian Life.

The difference between Christian Living and Christian Life is not so difficult to understand.

Christian Living

Christian Living aims at redefining Christianity with steps, procedures, and stories in a manner that allows successful living.

Christian Life

Christian Life aims at redefining your understanding of life and the sovereignty of Christ in a manner that allows a successful application of Christianity.

Hopefully, with the Bible as your Church Book, you will begin to experience Christ-centered living instead of life-centered Christianity.

+ + +

I guess some people fear that, relying only on the Word, you will just get caught up in the Old ways and times and lose sight of today's reality. Those people have probably never spent too much time in the Word. Without a belief in the gift of Faith, I would agree that I am being a little circular here.

Incidentally, most Christians believe in the gift of Faith.

I hope.

How much tougher the idea of the Holy Spirit?

If we simply read and believed the words in the Bible, we would see that we have a teacher, the Holy Spirit, and that He will direct our prayers and lives in a way that will allow us to ask the right questions and make the right observations.

But maybe you are feeling exploited with false words from the greedy.

Nevertheless, it is because we do not read the Bible that we believe the weak reality presented in the Christian Living section.

Q. Why are Stupid Church Books authors making the Bible appear as if it still needs interpreted or Christian Life appear so complex?
A. Why, because it is profitable, of course.

But why is it profitable?

It is profitable because the masses continue to see some greater value in *these* books beyond what they already have in their own hands.

They choose old bloody rags over fresh new undies.

You see, we Stupid Church Book authors are simply the bridge. We only say what your itching ears want to hear.

It is profitable for one reason only.

It is profitable because of **you** — the consumer.

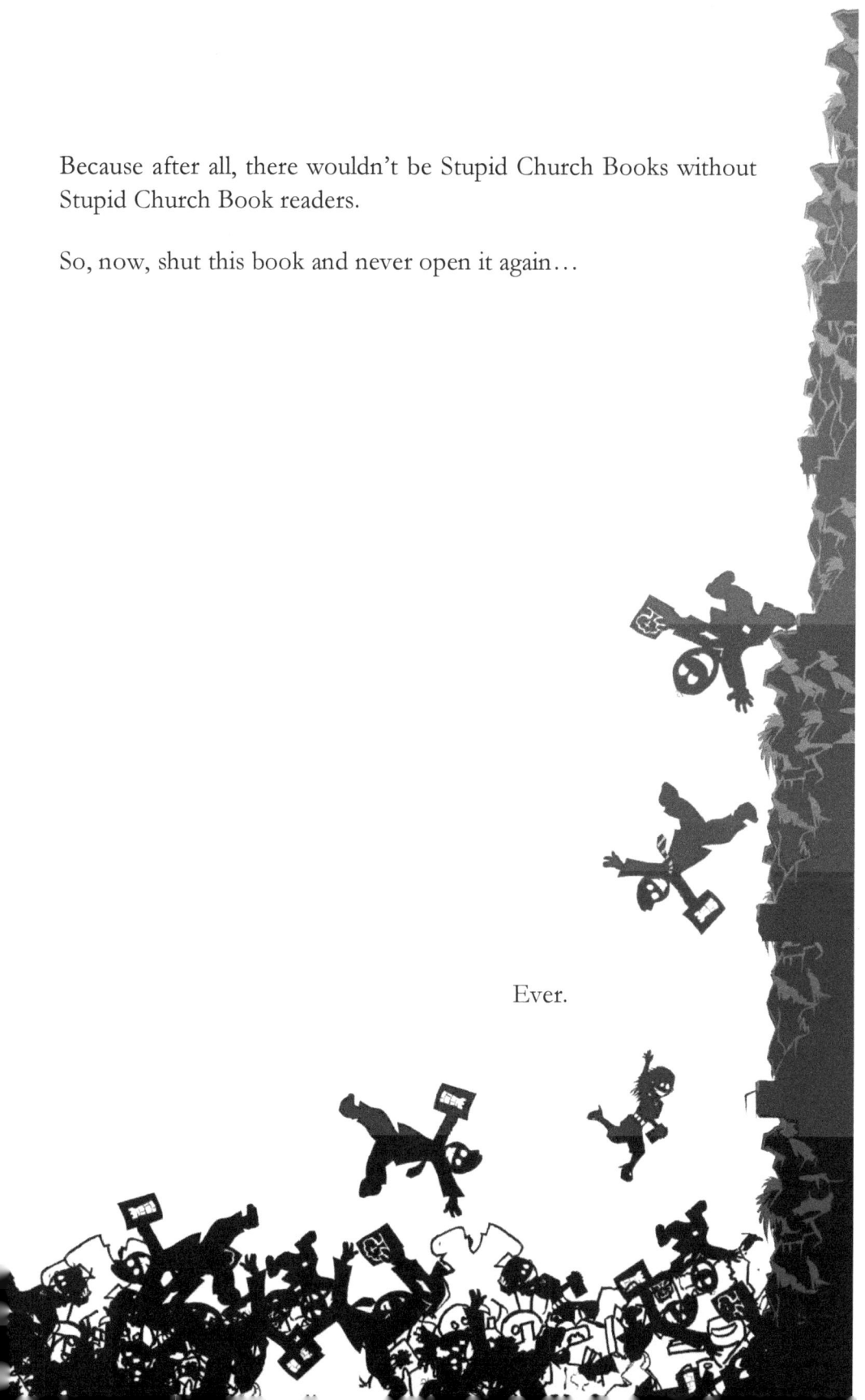

Because after all, there wouldn't be Stupid Church Books without Stupid Church Book readers.

So, now, shut this book and never open it again…

Ever.

ABOUT THE AUTHORS

In addition to his role as a Stupid Church Book author, Benjamin Samples (Ben) is the President & CEO of Project Management Consulting Services and Co-Founder of SCB Press. He graduated from West Virginia University with degrees in Mechanical and Aerospace Engineering and is a master's candidate in Engineering Management. Ben is an Army veteran and enjoys riding motorcycles and flying light aircraft. He lives with his wife, Nadya, in South Charleston, WV.

James Townsend, Co-Founder of SCB Press, is a writer, public speaker and musician. As a religious commentator, he hosts the popular podcast *Culture vs. Christian* and co-moderates the online Christian community of the same name. (Don't be the last to check it out at www.cultureversuschristian.com.) You can find James talking philosophy and drinking iced chai lattes at any of a number fine establishments around his home city of South Charleston, WV.

OUR ILLUSTRATOR

Austin Boyd, illustrator, editor, and marketing director of *The Last Stupid Church Book You'll Ever Read*, has over ten years experience in interactive marketing design and public relations. A graduate of West Virginia Wesleyan College, he holds a bachelors degree in Graphic Design. Austin resides in South Charleston, WV, with his family where he enjoys mountain biking, fly fishing, oil painting and photography as hobbies.

CHECK US OUT ON THE WEB!

The Last Stupid Church Book You'll Ever Read
is on the World Wide Web at:

www.stupidchurchbook.com

The Last Stupid Church Book You'll Ever Read
is a production of Stupid Church Book Press

SCB

STUPID CHURCH BOOK PRESS

CHARLESTON

www.ingramcontent.com/pod-product-compliance
Lightning Source LLC
Chambersburg PA
CBHW060243050426
42448CB00009B/1564